West's Law School Advisory Board

Global Issues in Corporate Law

By

Franklin A. Gevurtz
Distinguished Professor and Scholar
University of the Pacific,
McGeorge School of Law

AMERICAN CASEBOOK SERIES®

THOMSON

™

WEST

Mat #40347842

American Casebook Series and West Group are trademarks
registered in the U.S. Patent and Trademark Office.

© 2006 Thomson/West
      610 Opperman Drive
      P.O. Box 64526
      St. Paul, MN 55164–0526
      1–800–328–9352

Printed in the United States of America

ISBN–13: 978–0–314–15977–9
ISBN–10: 0–314–15977–0

TEXT IS PRINTED ON 10% POST
CONSUMER RECYCLED PAPER

To Carmen, Sara, Marvin and Manya

*

Preface

This book is designed primarily to serve as a supplement allowing professors teaching corporate law courses in law schools in the United States to introduce their students to corporate laws outside of the United States. By doing so, this book seeks to accomplish four goals:

The first is to **familiarize** students with foreign corporate laws. In a global economy, in which corporations formed under laws of other nations are key players, it is helpful for future lawyers to have some familiarity with the corporate laws under which such firms operate. Indeed, among the materials in this book are cases decided in courts in the United States, in which United States nationals, who were shareholders or creditors of corporations formed outside of the United States, found their rights governed by foreign corporate laws. Of course, one cannot expect law students to learn all of the variations in corporate laws around the world—any more than one can expect students to learn all of the corporate laws among the 50 states in the United States. Rather, starting with the first chapter in the book, which gives students a broad introduction to the basic business forms found worldwide, the book seeks to give the students a conceptual framework in which they can work as issues arise.

The second goal is to **clarify** United States corporate law. Many times, the best way to understand a particularly difficult area of law is to step back and examine how other systems address the same concerns. Take, for example, the doctrine of piercing the corporate veil. This is one of the most befuddled areas of corporate law, in which judicial substitution of rubric for functional analysis has confused generations of law students, not to mention lawyers and judges. Without meaning to suggest that other nations necessarily have superior law to the United States in this field, examination of various creditor protection rules found outside of the United States clarifies the fundamental concerns in ways that can take years to distill (as I confess it did for me) from reading just United States source material.

The third goal is to **challenge** students' unquestioning assumption that the law du jour in the United States is, by definition, the best law. For example, the European Union insider trading and takeover directives adopt approaches squarely rejected by courts in the United States, while German co-determination contravenes the assumption that only shareholders should elect directors. Showing students that other nations somehow function with corporate laws at odds with those in the United States helps create law school graduates with the openness of mind and imagination necessary for quality lawyering.

The fourth goal is to **predict** the direction of corporate law in the future. While legal education examines the law in the past and present, in the end, our graduates will deal with the law in the future. The history of corporate law is a history of migration of structures and rules from one nation to another—whether that is the spread of the European idea of a governing board, the German idea of the limited liability company, or the United States' idea of prohibiting insider trading. Examination of other nations' corporate laws will better enable future lawyers to anticipate where corporate law in the United States might go during the course of their careers.

On a practical note, this book is designed to work as a supplement, within the constraints this entails. It is short. It paints with a broad brush. The goal is to have the students gain a sense for the general concepts—*e.g.*, what are the fundamental areas of convergence (use of the board of directors) and divergence (co-determination, two-tier boards) in corporate governance—rather than drowning students in details (say, the use of independent directors in China). Whenever possible, the book contains materials that can substitute for materials the students would otherwise read (as, for example, by using United States court cases seeking to pierce the corporate veil of foreign corporations). The book is self-contained. The notes and text include all of the background reading necessary to understand the cases and other materials. Finally, each chapter, and even each section within the longer chapters, is designed to stand on its own—allowing professors to cover only some of the chapters or sections, and to cover them in different orders, depending upon the professors' overall organization of the course. (Various suggestions for use of these materials are found in the teachers' manual for this book.)

Regarding mechanics, certain conventions are followed in the preparation of this book. Citations in cases have been deleted without reference to the deletion. The English translations of the non-English statutes and court opinions found within this book are intended solely for educational purposes and can by no means be considered official. Umlauts, accent marks and similar symbols have been dropped from foreign words reprinted in this book. (Given the spelling of my last name as Gevurtz, rather than

Gewürz, I have standing to say that this was done for convenience, rather than as a sign of cultural disrespect.)

A number of persons aided in the preparation of this work. Thanks go to David Donald and Katharina Pistor for help on German law and, along with Alexander Klauser and Klaus Linke, for translating portions of the Mannesmann case; to Jon Lucchese for research, and for trying to put my foreign source citations in some semblance of generally accepted format; to Clemence George for research and translation of French language sources; and to Winfried van den Muijsenbergh and James McCahery for help with some questions on Dutch law. More broadly, thanks are due to my colleagues, who are participating in writing other books in this Global Issues series, and to Louis Higgins, of Thomson-West, for his enthusiastic support of this effort to "globalize" legal education in the United States.

*

Acknowledgements

Portions of the following copyrighted works are reprinted by permission:

Carston Alting, *Piercing the Corporate Veil in American and German Law—Liability of Individuals and Entities: A Comparative View*, 2 Tulsa J. Comp. & Int'l L. 187 (1995).

Rene Reich-Graefe, *Changing Paradigms: The Liability of Corporate Groups in Germany*, 37 Conn. L. Rev. 785 (2005).

Franklin A. Gevurtz, *The European Origins and Spread of the Corporate Board of Directors*, 33 Stetson L. Rev. 925 (2004).

Brian R. Cheffins, *Corporate Governance: Lessons from Australia*, 16 Transnat'l Law. 13 (2002).

Brian E. Aronson, *Learning from Comparative Law in Teaching U.S. Corporate Law: 1. Director's Liability in Japan and the U.S.*, 22 Penn. St. Int'l L. Rev. 213 (2003).

Andreas Cahn & David C. Donald, COMPARATIVE COMPANY LAW (forthcoming).

John Lyons, *Mexico Moves to Tighten Laws over Securities*, Wall Street Journal A14 (December 8, 2005).

Johnson, La Porta, Lopez-de-Silanes & Shleifer, *Tunneling*, 90 Am. Econ. Rev. 22 (2000).

Franklin A. Gevurtz, *The Globalization of Insider Trading Prohibitions*, 15 Transnat'l Law. 63 (2002).

Marco Ventoruzzo, *Europe's Thirteenth Directive and U.S. Takeover Regulation: Regulatory Means and Political and Economic Ends*, 41 Tex. Int'l L. Rev. 171 (2006).

*

Global Issues Series

Series Editor, Franklin A. Gevurtz

Available for Fall 2006 Classes

Global Issues in Civil Procedure by Thomas Main, University of the Pacific, McGeorge School of Law
ISBN 0–314–15978–9

Global Issues in Corporate Law by Franklin A. Gevurtz, University of the Pacific, McGeorge School of Law
ISBN 0–314–15977–0

Global Issues in Property Law by John G. Sprankling, University of the Pacific, McGeorge School of Law, Raymond R. Coletta, University of the Pacific, McGeorge School of Law, and M.C. Mirow, Florida International University College of Law
ISBN 0–314–16729–3

For Spring 2007 adoption, we also expect to have titles available in Contracts, Criminal Law, Labor Law, and Professional Responsibility.

*

Summary of Contents

*

Table of Contents

_____

Table of Cases

The principal cases are in bold type. Cases cited or discussed in the text
are roman type. References are to pages. Cases cited in principal
cases and within other quoted materials are not included.

Global Issues in Corporate Law

*

Chapter I

COMPANY TYPOLOGY

A quick survey of the names in a number of the principal court opinions found in casebooks used to teach Civil Procedure in law schools in the United States turned up the following:

Asahi Metal Industry Co., Ltd *v. Superior Court*

CIBC Mellon Trust Co. v. **Mora Hotel Corp. N.V.**

Granfinanciera, S.A. *v. Nordberg*

Holt v. **Klosters Rederi A/S**

LASA Per L'Industria Del Marmo Societa Per Azioni of Lasa, Italy *v. Alexander*

Volkswagenwerk Aktiengesellschaft *v. Schlunk*

What are the entities with such unusual suffixes in their names that are parties to these cases? From the surrounding context one deduces that these appear to be foreign examples of what we have grown used to calling corporations. Yet, the proliferation of lettering at the end of business names in the United States—*e.g.*, "L.L.C.", "L.L.P."—suggests perhaps the need for a little care before lumping all of this together in the corporate basket.

Interestingly, some decades ago, use of the term "corporation" (or its non-English language equivalent) to describe a business entity was largely confined to the United States. Persons in other nations spoke of "company" in English, or the foreign language equivalents to company— such as "*societe*" in French, "*sociedad*" in Spanish, "*gesellschaft*" in German, "*Vennootschap*" in Dutch, or "*kaisha*" in Japanese. The term company, or its non-English language equivalent, still figures in the legal description of foreign corporations, even if, under United States influence, the word corporation has found increasing use in common parlance.

The term company and its non-English language equivalents, however, encompass forms of business beyond that which one would consider to be a corporation. For example, it encompasses the ordinary commercial partnership (or *societe en nom collectif* in French, *offene Handelsge-*

sellschaft in German, or *gomei kaisha* in Japanese). Discussion of ordinary commercial partnerships is beyond the scope of a book on "Global Issues in Corporate Law." Suffice it to say that the laws in different nations governing the ordinary commercial partnership share universal agreement on key points. These include recognition of the ordinary commercial partnership as the default form for a business with more than one owner when the owners have not created some other form of business, as well as unlimited personal liability of the owners for the debts of the business. *E.g.*, Erik P.M. Vermeulen, *Network Effects and Regulatory Competition: An Introduction to the Expectations and Challenges of Partnership Law Reform*, (October 2005), TILEC Discussion Paper No. 2005–028, available at SSRN: http://ssrn.com/abstract=821885.

The limited partnership (or *societe en commandite simple* in French, *Kommanditgesellschaft* in German, or *goshi kaisha* in Japanese) is another form of company found in nations around the world. Indeed, this form of business started in medieval Italy, from which it spread to France, and then made its way to the United States. The fairly universal concept traditionally behind the limited partnership is that one or more of the company's owners will have both the power to control the venture and unlimited personal liability for the debts of the business, while other owners will simply be passive investors and will not be personally liable for the debts of the business (in other words, will have limited liability). S.N. Frommel & J.H. Thompson, COMPANY LAW IN EUROPE 88, 130, 183, 240–43, 296–97, 383, 435–36, 481, 546 (1975); Shoho [Commercial Code], arts. 146–64. Again, however, the limited partnership does not come within the scope of what is commonly meant when one refers to a corporation.

When one thinks of a corporation—or more precisely a business, as opposed to a municipal or non-profit, corporation—several attributes come to mind. The attribute from which the corporation derives this name (from "corpus" as in body) is legal treatment of the corporation as a person, with rights to hold property and be a party to a lawsuit. Limited liability for all of the owners and managers in the business is a second attribute commonly attributed to the corporation. Interestingly, however, limited liability for the owners was not a universally existing feature of corporations throughout much of their history, while laws governing partnerships have increasingly treated such firms as persons for legal purposes and, recently in the United States and England, begun to allow all owners of such firms to enjoy limited liability.

In fact, a third attribute associated with the corporation accounts for much of the worldwide spread of this business form, and explains the terminology in, and the structure of, many countries' corporate law. This attribute is the characterization of the owners of the business as stockholders or shareholders, who own fungible and tradeable interests in the company. Indeed, so critical has been this attribute, that many nations have used the label joint stock, or just stock, company (or the non-English language equivalent), instead of corporation, to describe this business form. (The term joint stock comes from the fact that, in the earliest of these companies, the merchant members in the companies chipped in money to buy a common stock of goods for trade (the joint stock), instead of each merchant trading on his own under the company's franchise. Gradually, the contributions to the joint trading stock evolved into investments in a permanent capital of the company, and the merchant members of the company evolved into the owners of the shares of this permanent capital (which continued for some time to be called the joint stock). The development of trading in these shares completed the creation of the joint stock company, or business corporation.)

The ability of the joint stock company to raise money through the sale of marketable shares of stock turned out to be a powerful tool for financing large business ventures, such as railroads. It also resulted in a number of historic financial scandals, from the bubble involving the so-called South Sea Company, all the way to Enron. The reaction in many countries was to subject the joint stock company to extensive requirements in its formation and operation. At the same time, owners of businesses began to appreciate the advantage of limiting their liability through use of the corporation or joint stock company, even if they planned to keep ownership closely held among a few individuals. The differential needs for regulation of businesses that would issue marketable stock, versus those that would be closely held, led to a split in approaches between different nations, and accounts for much of the typology encapsulated in the suffixes of foreign corporate names.

Germany pioneered an approach that is prevalent among civil law countries in Europe and elsewhere. In 1870, Germany enacted a statute allowing the creation of so-called stock companies (the *Atkiengesellschaft*, or AG). This statute, especially after an 1884 revision to cure abuses, is heavily regulatory. Deeming such a heavily regulatory approach unnecessary for companies without marketable stock, Germany enacted a second statute in 1892 allowing the formation of so-called companies with limited liability (the *Gesellschaft mit beschrankter Haftung* or GmbH), with less regulation. The German approach of separate laws for two types of corporations—one that could issue marketable stock (referred to throughout this book as a marketable stock company), and other that would enjoy the corporate attribute of limited liability for all owners but would not issue marketable stock (referred to throughout this book as a private company)—eventually spread throughout continental Europe, Latin America, as well as Japan. *E.g.*, Marcus Lutter, *Limited Liability Companies and Private Companies*, in XIII INTERNATIONAL ENCYCLOPEDIA OF COMPARATIVE LAW 4–5, 8 (1998).

The fundamental difference between the two types of corporations under the German system traditionally is that the private company cannot offer stock to the public, list shares for trading on the stock market, or even, significantly, issue negotiable share certificates, whereas the marketable stock company can. *E.g.*, Frommel & Thompson, *supra* at 19. Interestingly, this is not a difference for which there is an exact parallel in corporate law in the United States. Since the legal difference does not generally focus on the number of shareholders, the private company is not necessarily the same as a closely held or close corporation in United States corporate terminology. Because the differentiation between the marketable share company and the private company includes the ability issue negotiable share certificates, the marketable share company encompasses firms that would not always be a public corporation in United States corporate terminology.

Not only is it difficult to draw a precise parallel between the private and marketable share company, and corporate typology in the United States, the labels given to these business forms in nations that use them are not entirely helpful. For example, the German label *Gesellschaft mit beschrankter Haftung* (GmbH)—literally, company with limited liability, but often translated as limited liability company—hardly distinguishes the private GmbH from the marketable share AG, since both forms provide their owners with limited liability. Nevertheless, the label "company with limited liability" (or, more accurately, the non-English language equivalent) has become the accepted designation for this form of business, so that such a firm is called a

> *societe a responsabilite limitee* (the SARL) in French,
>
> *sociedad de responsabilidad limitada* (the SRL or SL) in Spanish,
>
> *societa a responsabilita limitata* (the Srl) in Italian,
>
> *besloten vennootschap met beperkte aansprakelijkheid* (the BV) in Dutch,
>
> *anpartsselskab* (the Aps) in Danish, and
>
> *yugen kaisha* in Japanese.

The designations for the marketable stock company display greater variation even in their English language equivalents. The German label *Atkiengesellschaft* (AG)—literally stock company—presumably tries to capture the notion that such firms alone can issue negotiable stock. Choosing instead to focus on the lack of an owner's name in the company name, the French refer to the marketable stock company as a *societe anonyme* (the SA). Other nations generally follow one of these two approaches, so that the designation for the marketable stock company is a

> *Aktieselskab* (the A/S) in Danish,
>
> *Aktiebolag* (the A/B) in Swedish,
>
> *sociedad anonima* (the SA) in Spanish,
>
> *societa per azioni* (the SpA) in Italian,
>
> *Naamloze Vennootschap* (the NV) in Dutch, and
>
> *kabushiki kaisha* in Japanese.

England, the United States, and other common law countries traditionally did not follow the German approach of having two entirely different statutory schemes for two different types of corporations. Instead, common law jurisdictions typically worked with one basic statute for all business corporations—known in England as a company limited by shares—with additional legislative or judicially-created special rules for closely held or private companies at one extreme, and for companies selling stock to the public or listing shares for trading on an exchange at the other extreme. For example, in England, and English commonwealth countries, special provisions in the company law traditionally limited disclosure requirements for so-called private companies. *E.g.*, Lutter *supra* at 7–8.

The advent of the limited liability company in the United States suggests a growing influence for the German two types of corporation approach—albeit, tax considerations, rather than the different regulatory needs of businesses without marketable stock, led to the establishment of the limited liability company in the United States. In England, the need to comply with European Council directives designed to harmonize the corporate laws of European Union member nations—which directives tend to reflect the German two types of corporations—has led to significant modification of the English law, moving its results, if not terminology and structure, toward the German dichotomy.

Chapter II

CHOICE OF LAW

A central feature of the global economy is the existence of corporations formed in one nation, but doing business in other nations. Whose corporate laws govern such firms?

McDERMOTT INCORPORATED v. LEWIS

531 A.2d 206 (Del. 1987).

We confront an important issue of first impression—whether a Delaware subsidiary of a Panamanian corporation may vote the shares it holds in its parent company under circumstances which are prohibited by Delaware law, but not the law of Panama. Necessarily, this involves questions of foreign law, and applicability of the internal affairs doctrine under Delaware law.

Plaintiffs, Harry Lewis and Nina Altman, filed these consolidated suits in the Court of Chancery in December, 1982 seeking to enjoin or rescind the 1982 Reorganization under which McDermott Incorporated, a Delaware corporation ("McDermott Delaware"), became a 92%-owned subsidiary of McDermott International, Inc., a Panamanian corporation ("International"). Lewis and Altman are stockholders of McDermott Delaware, which emerged from the Reorganization owning approximately 10% of International's common stock. Plaintiffs challenged this aspect of the Reorganization, and the Court of Chancery granted partial summary judgment in their favor, holding that McDermott Delaware could not vote its stock in International.

* * *

I.

International was incorporated in Panama on August 11, 1959, and is principally engaged in providing worldwide marine construction services to the oil and gas industry. Its executive offices are in New Orleans, Louisiana, and there are no operations in Delaware. International does not maintain offices in Delaware, hold meetings or conduct business here, have agents or employees in Delaware, or have any assets here.

McDermott Delaware and its subsidiaries operate throughout the United States in three principal industry segments: marine construction services, power generation systems and equipment, and engineered materials. McDermott Delaware's principal offices are in New Orleans.

Following the 1982 Reorganization, McDermott Delaware became a 92%-owned subsidiary of International. The public stockholders of International hold approximately 90% of the voting power of International, while McDermott Delaware holds about 10%.

The stated "principal purpose" of the reorganization, according to International's prospectus, was to enable the McDermott Group to retain, reinvest and redeploy earnings from operations outside the United States without subjecting such earnings to United States income tax. The prospectus also admitted that the 10% voting interest given to McDermott Delaware would be voted by International, "and such voting power could be used to oppose an attempt by a third party to acquire control of International if the management of International believes such use of the voting power would be in the best interests of the stockholders of International." An exchange offer [under which McDermott Delaware stockholders exchanged their stock for shares in International], and thus the Reorganization, was supported by 89.59% of McDermott Delaware stockholders.

The applicable Panamanian law is set forth in the record by affidavits and opinion letters of Ricardo A. Durling, Esquire, and the deans of two Panamanian law schools, to support the claim that McDermott Delaware's retention of a 10% interest in International, and its right to vote those shares, is permitted by the laws of Panama. Significantly, the plaintiffs have not offered any contrary evidence.

* * *

[According to McDermott Delaware's experts, Panamanian law does not prohibit a subsidiary of a Panamanian corporation from voting shares the subsidiary owns in the parent corporation unless the Panamanian corporation registered its shares for trading within Panama with the National Securities Commission of Panama. While the case was awaiting decision by the Delaware Supreme Court, International registered— thereby precluding McDermott Delaware from being able to vote the shares it owned in International in the future.] This change in circumstances technically renders the appeal moot. Normally, we decline to decide moot issues. * * * Given the importance of this matter to Delaware corporation law, and the state in which it otherwise would be left, we are compelled to decide this case based on the facts presented to the trial court.

II.

We note at the outset that if International were incorporated either in Delaware or Louisiana, its stock could not be voted by a majority-owned subsidiary. No United States jurisdiction of which we are aware permits that practice.

* * *

III.

* * *

Corporations and individuals alike enter into contracts, commit torts, and deal in personal and real property. * * * The internal affairs doctrine has no applicability in these situations. Rather, this doctrine governs the choice of law determinations involving matters peculiar to corporations, that is, those activities concerning the relationships inter se of the corporation, its directors, officers and shareholders.

The internal affairs doctrine requires that the law of the state of incorporation should determine issues relating to internal corporate affairs. * * *

A.

Delaware's well established conflict of laws principles require that the laws of the jurisdiction of incorporation—here the Republic of Panama—govern this dispute involving McDermott International's voting rights.

* * *

However, in *Western Air Lines, Inc. v. Sobieski*, 191 Cal.App.2d 399, 12 Cal.Rptr. 719 (1961), a California court upheld an order of the California Commissioner of Corporations directing a Delaware corporation having major contacts with California to follow the cumulative voting requirements imposed by California law. After the *Western Air* decision, commentators noted that the case signaled the alleged start of a "conflicts revolution." * * *

A review of cases over the last twenty-six years, however, finds that in all but a few, the law of the state of incorporation was applied without any discussion. * * *

B.

Given the significance of these considerations, application of the internal affairs doctrine is not merely a principle of conflicts law. It is also one of serious constitutional proportions—under due process, the commerce clause and the full faith and credit clause—so that the law of one state governs the relationships of a corporation to its stockholders, directors and officers in matters of internal corporate governance. The alternatives present almost intolerable consequences to the corporate enterprise and its managers. With the existence of multistate and multinational organizations, directors and officers have a significant right, under the fourteenth amendment's due process clause, to know what law will be applied to their actions. Stockholders also have a right to know by what standards of accountability they may hold those managing the corporation's business and affairs. That is particularly so here, given the significant fact that in the McDermott Group reorganization, and after full disclosure, 89.59% of the total outstanding common shares of McDermott Delaware were tendered in the exchange offer. Thus, by an overwhelming choice those stockholders received shares in International, and thereby selected the laws of Panama to govern inter se the corporate relations between themselves, International, its directors, officers and agents. Such issues have been the subject of litigation and scholarly discussions for decades. However, an attitude has developed in some quarters which exalts local interests over more fundamental doctrines. We approach such teachings with reservations.

Under the commerce clause *Pike v. Bruce Church, Inc.*, 397 U.S. 137, 142, 90 S.Ct. 844, 847, 25 L.Ed.2d 174 (1970), determined that a state may regulate interstate commerce indirectly, but emphasized that the burden placed upon interstate commerce may not be excessive in relation to the local interests served by the regulation. In *Edgar v. MITE Corp.*, 457 U.S. 624, 102 S.Ct. 2629, 73 L.Ed.2d 269 (1982), the Supreme Court ruled that under the commerce clause a state "has no interest in regulating the internal affairs of foreign corporations." If that is so, then a court or state which attempts to displace the internal affairs doctrine carries a heavy burden to justify its actions.

The recent decision in *CTS Corp. v. Dynamics Corp. of America*, 481 U.S. 69, 107 S.Ct. 1637, 95 L.Ed.2d 67 (1987), seems to support this interpretation of *MITE*:

> This Court's recent Commerce Clause cases also have invalidated statutes that adversely may affect interstate commerce by subjecting activities to inconsistent regulations ... The Indiana Act poses no such problem. So long as each State regulates voting rights only in the corporations it has created, each corporation will be subject to the law of only one state. No principal of corporation law and practice is more firmly established than a State's authority to regulate domestic corporations, including the authority to define the voting rights of shareholders ... This beneficial free market system depends at its core upon the fact that a corporation—except in the rarest situations—is organized under, and governed by, the law of a single jurisdiction, traditionally the corporate law of the state of its incorporation.

Thus, we conclude that application of the internal affairs doctrine is mandated by constitutional principles, except in "the rarest situations."

* * *

[A]pplication of [Delaware's corporate law] to International would violate the commerce clause. * * * For Delaware now to interfere in the internal affairs of a foreign corporation having no relationship whatever to this State clearly implies that International can be subjected to the differing laws of all fifty states on various matters respecting its internal affairs. * * *

IV.

Plaintiffs protest the issuance of voting stock to McDermott Delaware on public policy grounds, relying on the following statement from *Norlin* [*Corp. v. Rooney, Pace Inc.*, 744 F.2d 255 (2d Cir.1984)]:

> [The] statutes seek to safeguard minority shareholders from management attempts at self-perpetuation. If cross-ownership and cross-voting of stock between parents and subsidiaries were unregulated, officers and directors could easily entrench themselves by exchanging a sufficient number of shares to block any challenge to their autonomy. . . .

* * * But here, we are called upon to apply the laws of Panama to a Panamanian corporation having no contacts with Delaware.

* * *

In conclusion, the trial court erred as a matter of law in ignoring the uncontroverted Panamanian law, and in applying Delaware and/or Louisiana law to the internal affairs of International contrary to established Delaware law and important constitutional principles. Accordingly the judgment of the Court of Chancery is REVERSED.

Notes

1. The court's holding in *McDermott* suggests that attorneys in the United States might need to become familiar with foreign corporate laws. Why was the relevant corporate law that of Panama (International's nation of incorporation) rather than Delaware (McDermott Delaware's state of incorporation)? Which company's internal affairs were at issue in this case?

2. The transaction in *McDermott* pioneered the so-called "inversion" or "expatriation," in which a Delaware parent corporation and its non-United States subsidiary corporation switch roles—so that the Delaware corporation becomes the subsidiary, while the non-United States corporation becomes the parent—in order to reduce United States income taxes paid by the corporate group on its worldwide income. Other corporations, starting in the mid–1990s, followed suit. By the 2004 election year, the growing trend lead to complaints about disloyal corporations that became foreign in order to reduce their United States taxes in a time of war. In response, Congress amended the tax law to treat the foreign parent as a United States corporation for income tax purposes. I.R.C. § 7874(b) (as enacted by the American Jobs Creation Act of 2004).

3. The next case is a decision by the European Court of Justice involving provisions of the European Community Treaty. The legal structure governing what is now referred to as the European Union can be very difficult to fully understand. For present purposes, however, a grossly oversimplified description should suffice.

The European Union is the upshot of a series of treaties going all the way back to the Treaty of Paris of 1951 (which established the European Coal and Steel Community), to the two Treaties of Rome of 1957 (one of which established the European Atomic Energy Community, and the other of which, most significantly of all, established the European Economic Community (the EEC, now just referred to as the European Community or EC)), through the 1993 Maastricht Treaty on European Union, and so on. The combined resulting governing document is referred to as the European Community (or EC) Treaty.

The EC Treaty establishes a number of governing bodies, including the European Council (comprised of representatives picked by the government of each member nation with the clear understanding that they are to represent the interests of their national governments), the European Commission (the members of which are to be independent of, even though nominated by, their national governments), and the European Parliament (directly elected by the people of the member nations). In fact, the European Council has the principal legislative authority, with the European Commission playing the role of proposing and implementing legislation, and the European Parliament playing a complex role in which its support of, or opposition to, legislation changes the requirements for adoption of the legislation by the European Council. The European Council enacts a couple of different types of legislation. "Regulations" are legislation that directly act as law, in the sense that national courts must apply them as relevant and they can create rights and liabilities for individuals. By contrast, "directives" are orders to the national legislatures in the member nations and require implementing national legislation.

The European Court of Justice (or ECJ) exists by virtue of the EC Treaty to "ensure that in the interpretation and application of this Treaty the law is observed." Of most relevance for European Union corporate law, the ECJ can hear claims brought by the European Commission against member nations for failure to comply with treaty obligations, and can provide rulings, at the request of the national courts of European Union members, on the interpretation and application of EC Treaty provisions.

KAMER VAN KOOPHANDEL EN FABRIEKEN VOOR AMSTERDAM v. INSPIRE ART LTD.

Case C–167/01, 2003 E.C.R. I–10155 (European Court of Justice 2003).

* * *

I—The legal framework

The relevant provisions of Community law

The first paragraph of Article 43 EC [Treaty] provides:

> Within the framework of the provisions set out below, restrictions on the freedom of establishment of nationals of a Member State in the territory of another Member State shall be prohibited. Such prohibition shall also apply to restrictions on the setting-up of agencies, branches or subsidiaries by nationals of any Member State established in the territory of any Member State.

Article 48 EC extends entitlement to freedom of establishment, subject to the same conditions as those laid down for individuals who are nationals of the Member States, to "companies or firms formed in accordance with the law of a Member State and having their registered office, central administration or principal place of business within the Community".

Article 46 EC permits the Member States to restrict the freedom of establishment of foreign nationals by adopting "provisions laid down by law, regulation or administrative action", in so far as such provisions are justified "on grounds of public policy, public security or public health".

Article 44(2)(g) EC empowers the Council of the European Union, for the purpose of giving effect to freedom of establishment, to coordinate "to the necessary extent the safeguards which, for the protection of the interests of members and others, are required by Member States of companies or firms within the meaning of the second paragraph of Article 48 of the EC Treaty with a view to making such safeguards equivalent throughout the Community."

Various directives have in that manner been adopted by the Council on that basis ("company-law directives") and, in particular, the following directives referred to in the dispute in the main proceedings.

* * *

The Eleventh Council Directive [specifies] * * * disclosure requirements in respect of branches opened in a Member State by certain types of company governed by the law of another State.

* * *

According to the fifth recital in the preamble to [the Eleventh] directive "in this field the differences in the laws of the Member States may interfere with the exercise of the right of establishment ... [and] it is therefore necessary to eliminate such differences in order to safeguard, inter alia, the exercise of that right".

* * *

The relevant provisions of national [Netherlands] law

Article 1 of the [Wet op de Formeel Buitenlandse Vennotschappen (Law on Formally Foreign Companies) of 17 December 1997 (the "WFBV")] defines a "formally foreign company" as "a capital company formed under laws other than those of the Netherlands and having legal personality, which carries on its activities entirely or almost entirely in the Netherlands and also does not have any real connection with the State within which the law under which the company was formed applies ... ".

Articles 2 to 5 of the WFBV impose on formally foreign companies various obligations concerning the company's registration in the commercial register, an indication of that status in all the documents produced by it, the minimum share capital and the drawing-up, production and publication of the annual documents. The WFBV also provides for penalties in case of non-compliance with those provisions.

In particular, Article 2 of the WFBV requires a company falling within the definition of a formally foreign company to be registered as such in the commercial register [in the Netherlands].

* * *

Pursuant to Article 4(1) of the WFBV, the subscribed capital of a formally foreign company must be at least equal to the minimum amount required of Netherlands limited companies by Article 2:178 of the * * * Netherlands Civil Code, which was EUR 18,000 on 1 September 2000. * * *

Until the conditions relating to capital and paid-up share capital have been satisfied, the directors are jointly and severally liable with the company for all legal acts carried out during their directorship which are binding on the company.

* * *

II—The dispute in the main proceedings and the questions referred for a preliminary ruling

Inspire Art was formed on 28 July 2000 in the legal form of a private company limited by shares under the law of England and Wales and it has its registered office at Folkestone (United Kingdom). Its sole director, whose domicile is in The Hague (Netherlands), is authorised to act alone and independently in the name of the company. The company, which carries on activity under the business name "Inspire Art Ltd" in the sphere of dealing in objets d'art, began trading on 17 August 2000 and has a branch in Amsterdam.

Inspire Art is registered in the commercial register of the Chamber of Commerce without any indication of the fact that it is a formally foreign company within the meaning of Article 1 of the WFBV.

Taking the view that that indication was mandatory on the ground that Inspire Art traded exclusively in the Netherlands, the Chamber of Commerce applied to the Kantongerecht te Amsterdam [a Netherlands court] on 30 October 2000 for an order that there should be added to that company's registration in the commercial register the statement that it is a formally foreign company, in accordance with Article 1 of the WFBV, which would entail other obligations laid down by law, set out * * * above.

Inspire Art denie[d, in the Netherlands court proceeding,] that its registration is incomplete, primarily because the company does not meet * * * [the definition of a formally foreign company within the meaning of] the WFBV. As a secondary point, if the Kantongerecht were to decide that it met [that definition], it maintained that the WFBV was contrary to Community law, and to Articles 43 EC and 48 EC in particular.

In its order of 5 February 2001 the Kantongerecht held that Inspire Art was a formally foreign company within the meaning of Article 1 of the WFBV.

As regards the compatibility of the WFBV with Community law, [the Netherlands court] decided to stay proceedings and refer the following questions to the Court of Justice for a preliminary ruling:

> Are Articles 43 EC and 48 EC to be interpreted as precluding the Netherlands, pursuant to the [WFBV], from attaching additional conditions, such as those laid down in Articles 2 to 5 of that law, to the establishment in the Netherlands of a branch of a company which has been set up in the United Kingdom with the sole aim of securing the advantages which that offers compared to incorporation under Netherlands law, given that Netherlands law imposes stricter rules than those applying in the United Kingdom with regard to the setting-up of companies and payment for shares, and given that the Netherlands law infers that aim from the fact that the company carries on its activities entirely or almost entirely in the Netherlands and, furthermore, does not have any real connection with the State in which the law under which it was formed applies?

* * *

[IV—] Consideration of the questions referred

* * *

[S]everal of the provisions of the WFBV fall within the scope of the Eleventh Directive, since that concerns disclosure requirements in respect of branches opened in a Member State by companies * * * governed by the law of another Member State.

* * *

[The court pointed out that while some of the disclosure requirements imposed by the WFBV on formally foreign corporations were consistent with the Eleventh Directive, some went beyond the disclosure called for by that directive.]

It is therefore necessary to consider, with regard to those obligations, whether the harmonisation brought about by the Eleventh Directive * * * is exhaustive.

* * *

[I]t follows from the * * * fifth recital in the preamble to the Directive that the differences in respect of branches between the laws of the Member States, especially as regards disclosure, may interfere with the exercise of the right of establishment and must therefore be eliminated.

* * *

It must therefore be concluded on this point that it is contrary to * * * the Eleventh Directive for national legislation such as the WFBV to impose on the branch of a company formed in accordance with the laws of another Member State disclosure obligations not provided for by that directive.

[S]everal of the provisions of the WFBV do not fall within the scope of the Eleventh Directive. Those are the rules relating to the minimum capital required, both at the time of registration and for so long as a formally foreign company exists, and those relating to the penalty attaching to non-compliance with the obligations laid down by the WFBV, namely, the joint and several liability of the directors with the company (Article 4(1) and (2) of the WFBV). Those provisions must therefore be considered in the light of Articles 43 EC and 48 EC.

* * *

The Court has held that it is immaterial, having regard to the application of the rules on freedom of establishment, that the company was formed in one Member State only for the purpose of establishing itself in a second Member State, where its main, or indeed entire, business is to be conducted. The reasons for which a company chooses to be formed in a particular Member State are, save in the case of fraud, irrelevant with regard to application of the rules on freedom of establishment (*Centros*).

* * *

Thus, in the main proceedings, the fact that Inspire Art was formed in the United Kingdom for the purpose of circumventing Netherlands company law which lays down stricter rules with regard in particular to minimum capital and the paying-up of shares does not mean that that company's establishment of a branch in the Netherlands is not covered by freedom of establishment as provided for by Articles 43 EC and 48 EC. * * *

The argument that freedom of establishment is not in any way infringed by the WFBV inasmuch as foreign companies are fully recognised in the Netherlands and are not refused registration in that Member State's business register, that law having the effect simply of laying down a number of additional obligations classified as "administrative", cannot be accepted.

* * *

The legislation at issue in the case in the main proceedings, which requires the branch of such a company formed in accordance with the legislation of a Member State to comply with the rules of the State of establishment on share capital and directors' liability, has the effect of impeding the exercise by those companies of the freedom of establishment conferred by the Treaty.

* * *

Whether there is any justification

* * *

It must first of all be stated that none of the arguments put forward by the Netherlands Government with a view to justifying the legislation at issue in the main proceedings falls within the ambit of Article 46 EC.

The justifications put forward by the Netherlands Government, namely, the aims of protecting creditors, combating improper recourse to freedom of establishment, and protecting both effective tax inspections and fairness in business dealings, fall therefore to be evaluated by reference to overriding reasons related to the public interest.

It must be borne in mind that, according to the Court's case-law, national measures liable to hinder or make less attractive the exercise of fundamental freedoms guaranteed by the Treaty must, if they are to be justified, fulfil four conditions: they must be applied in a non-discriminatory manner; they must be justified by imperative requirements in the public interest; they must be suitable for securing the attainment of the objective which they pursue, and they must not go beyond what is necessary in order to attain it.

In consequence, it is necessary to consider whether those conditions are fulfilled by provisions relating to minimum capital such as those at issue in the main proceedings.

First, with regard to protection of creditors, and there being no need for the Court to consider whether the rules on minimum share capital constitute in themselves an appropriate protection measure, it is clear that Inspire Art holds itself out as a company governed by the law of England and Wales and not as a Netherlands company. Its potential creditors are put on sufficient notice that it is covered by legislation other than that regulating the formation in the Netherlands of limited liability companies and, in particular, laying down rules in respect of minimum capital and directors' liability.

* * *

The answer to be given to the second question referred by the national court must therefore be that the impediment to the freedom of establishment guaranteed by the Treaty constituted by provisions of national law, such as those at issue, relating to minimum capital and the personal joint and several liability of directors cannot be justified under Article 46 EC, or on grounds of protecting creditors, or combating improper recourse to freedom of establishment or safeguarding fairness in business dealings or the efficiency of tax inspections.

In light of all the foregoing considerations, the answers to be given to the questions referred for a preliminary ruling must be:

> —It is contrary to Article 2 of the Eleventh Directive for national legislation such as the WFBV to impose on the branch of a company formed in accordance with the laws of another Member State disclosure obligations not provided for by that directive.

> —It is contrary to Articles 43 EC and 48 EC for national legislation such as the WFBV to impose on the exercise of freedom of secondary establishment in that State by a company formed in accordance with the law of another Member State certain conditions provided for in domestic company law in respect of company formation relating to minimum capital and directors' liability. The reasons for which the

company was formed in that other Member State, and the fact that it carries on its activities exclusively or almost exclusively in the Member State of establishment, do not deprive it of the right to invoke the freedom of establishment guaranteed by the EC Treaty, save where the existence of an abuse is established on a case-by-case basis.

* * *

KAISHA HOU [CORPORATIONS LAW] ART. 821

(Japan 2005).

Article 821 (Pseudo–Foreign Companies)

(1) A foreign company that has a head office in Japan, or whose principal purpose is the carrying on of business in Japan, may not continuously engage in transactions in Japan.

Any person who engages in transactions in violation of the provisions of the preceding paragraph shall, in relation to counterparties, be jointly and severally liable with the foreign company for repayment of any debts incurred as a result of such transactions.

Notes

1. *McDermott* and *Inspire Art* involve companies that incorporated in one nation and did business in another. In a global economy, this fact is unexceptional. These two cases involve something more, however, than a company doing business in a nation other than where it incorporated. In both cases, it appears that the companies conducted little or no business in (or had much of any other connection with) the nation of incorporation. Hence, the holdings in both *McDermott* and *Inspire Art* stand for the proposition that parties forming a corporation essentially can pick their corporate law from the menu of choices provided by other nations—regardless of where the company actually operates or where its shareholders reside. This has profound consequences from the standpoint of both lawyers advising clients and policy makers considering corporate regulation.

Not every jurisdiction accepts this notion of free choice of corporate law, as illustrated by Article 821 of Japan's newly redrafted corporation statute, as well as the California law applied by the *Wilson* decision criticized in *McDermott*. Actually, the Japanese statute and California law address this issue in two very different ways, in that each attacks a different legal leg upon which the free choice regime rests.

The first leg upon which the free choice regime rests is the notion that persons can form corporations in jurisdictions other than one in which the company will conduct operations. The notion that the mere filing of a piece of paper (combined with a nominal local address) dictates the nation (or state) of incorporation is often referred to the incorporation doctrine, and characterized as an Anglo–American view. By contrast, many continental European nations traditionally operated under the view that corporations must be formed in the nation in which the company had its headquarters—

variously called the *siege social, siege real,* or seat theory. Under this view, a nation would reject the effort to incorporate under its law if the corporate headquarters would be in another nation, and a nation in which a firm had its headquarters would refuse to recognize the firm as a corporation—meaning, for example, the firm would lack the capacity to sue in this nation's courts and its owners might face personal liability—unless the firm incorporated under this nation's, rather than another nation's, laws. *E.g.,* Wulf–Henning Roth, *From Centros to Uberseering: Free Movement of Companies, Private International Law, and Company Law,* 52 Int'l & Comp. L.Q. 177, 180–185 (2003). This is generally the approach taken by Japan's Article 821.

Both the Netherlands' statute dealing with "formally foreign corporations," and the California law applied in the *Wilson* case (specifically, a California statute dealing with "quasi foreign corporations"), attack the matter from the other leg. These laws recognize the existence of the foreign corporation, but, at least partially, reject the internal affairs rule in favor of applying various parts the corporate law of the nation (or state) that has more actual contacts with the corporation's activities and shareholders.

From a legal (rather than a policy) standpoint, a nation, like Japan, is at liberty to refuse to recognize the existence of foreign corporations whose activities are predominately within the nation, rather than where the company incorporated. Alternately, a nation can reject the internal affairs doctrine in favor of other choice-of-law principles. As the discussion in *McDermott,* and the result in *Inspire Art,* indicate, things change when states or nations are part of a federal system or linked by treaty regulating their economic activities.

A substantial motivation both for the United States Constitution, and for the treaties creating the European Union, was to eliminate barriers that the member states or nations had constructed to trade between themselves. Hence, it is not surprising that the governing documents in both cases contain provisions—the Commerce Clause in the case of the United States Constitution, the articles calling for freedom of establishment in the case of the EC Treaty—that the courts in *McDermott* and *Inspire Art* held to limit the ability of a state in the United States, or a nation in the European Union, to interfere with the free choice of corporate law.

When the United States Constitution was drafted, corporations were hardly the dominant business form that they are today. Hence, it is understandable why the Constitution contains no direct reference to regulation of corporations. By contrast, modern recognition of the important role of corporations resulted in Articles 43 and 48 of the EC Treaty, which expressly require member nations in the European Union to allow companies formed under the laws of other member nations to set up shop. *Inspire Art* is the third of a trilogy of cases by the ECJ, which applied these articles to situations in which Danish, German and Dutch nationals had formed English (or, ironically in the German case, Netherlands) companies to conduct business in their home countries. Simplifying the matter, the first two of these cases (Case C–212/97 *Centros Ltd. v. Erhvervs-og Selskabsstyrelsen,* 1999 E.C.R. I–1459, and Case C–208/00 *Uberseering BV v. Nordic Construction Co. Baumanagement,* 2002 E.C.R. I–9919) held that these articles compelled recognition of corporations formed under one member nation's law, despite the fact that the headquarters, business and owners of the company were all within the nation that refused to recognize the corporation. The result essentially is to prevent application of the seat theory, at least in the context of refusing to recognize corporations formed under the laws of European Union member nations following the incorporation doctrine. The Dutch law involved in *Inspire Art* sought to get around these results by recognizing the non-Dutch corporation, but seeking to apply certain parts of Dutch law. In this situation, how exactly does forcing such companies to live with the same law as Dutch corporations, interfere with freedom of establishment?

From a policy standpoint, notice that both *McDermott* and *Inspire Art* reflect a philosophy toward choice of law that sees nothing wrong with organizers of a corporation being able to choose in a "marketplace for competing laws" the law they find most attractive. Does this regime allow organizers to choose laws that prejudice shareholders (the Panamanian voting rules in *McDermott*) or creditors (the English minimum capital rules in *Inspire Art*) of the corporation? Does the fact, emphasized by the court in *McDermott*, that over 90 percent of the McDermott Delaware shareholders volunteered to trade their shares for stock in International—knowing that International was a Panama corporation and that Panama law would allow the subsidiary to vote its stock in the parent—eliminate this concern? Were there some reasons why the shareholders might have made the exchange—for example, fear of remaining a shareholder in a subsidiary—even if they did not care for Panamanian law. The court in *Inspire Art* extends this "protect yourself" approach to cast aside the Netherlands' concern for creditors of poorly capitalized English companies doing business in the Netherlands, by pointing out that the creditors will know that they are dealing with an English corporation. Is it realistic to expect that persons doing business with a gallery on a street in Amsterdam are going to be aware both of the gallery's nation of incorporation and of the capital rules provided by that nation's corporate law? (Incidentally, notice how the court in *Inspire Art* held that Article 46's "public policy" justification was entirely inapplicable; thereby forcing the Netherlands to defend the law against an apparently more demanding judicially-created "public interest" justification.)

2. Federal regimes not only can constrain member states to follow the corporate laws of other member states, but also can impose corporate laws adopted by the national government (in the case of the United States) or European governing bodies (in the case of the European Union). In the United States, the principal national "corporate" law comes from the 1933 Securities Act, and the 1934 Securities Exchange Act, as amended and supplemented particularly by the Williams Act in 1968 and the Sarbanes–Oxley Act in 2002. As discussed in *Inspire Art*, the principal European corporate law comes from the directives promulgated by the European Council pursuant to Article 44 of the EC Treaty.

There are several broad conceptual differences between the United States federal law in the corporate area provided by the securities laws, and the European corporate law provided by the European Council directives. The first is the purpose of the laws. As stated by the court in *Inspire Art*, the purpose of directives promulgated pursuant to Article 44 is to harmonize the disparate corporate laws in the member nations of the European Union in order to promote free establishment of corporations in member nations. By contrast, the purpose of the securities laws in the United States, for the most part, is not to promote any notion of uniformity for its own sake, but rather to address concerns Congress did not feel adequately dealt with under state law. Related to this difference in purpose is a difference in scope—the European Council harmonization directives cover a much broader range of corporate law topics than do the securities laws in the United States (the focus of which is principally on disclosure to investors). For example, the European Council directives actually cover the subject of minimum capital— but only for corporations with marketable stock, rather than for the sort of private companies involved in *Inspire Art*. Finally, as discussed earlier, directives (unlike the United States securities laws) do not in themselves have the effect of law; rather they are instructions to the legislatures of the member nations of the European Union as to what the national corporate legislation must contain.

The Eleventh European Council Directive created an issue in *Inspire Art* as to whether member nations could mandate more disclosure than the directive required to be in their corporate laws. Compare the court's interpretation of the Eleventh Directive, with Section 18(a) and (b) of the 1933 Securities Act (as amended), which preempt any state securities laws in the United States from requiring registration of so-called covered securities, but otherwise do not preempt state securities regulation. Actually, however, despite the goal of harmonization, and the court's interpretation of the Eleventh Directive to preclude more extensive disclosure requirements in the areas covered by the directive, corporate law within the European Union remains far from uniform. For one thing, the directives commonly contain options, or act as a floor above which member nations can impose higher standards, rather than, as the court interpreted the Eleventh Directive, creating one exclusive rule. *E.g.*, Vanessa Edwards, EC COMPANY LAW 10 (1999). In addition, the more fundamental the difference in corporate law— as, for example, the requirement in some European Union member nations that employees have the right to elect some members to the corporation's board (co-determination)—the more difficult it becomes to gain the necessary consensus in the European Council behind a directive. Hence, directives have not harmonized many of the more fundamental differences in European corporate laws.

A more extreme possibility for a central corporate law in a federal regime would be to have companies form under a national (as opposed to a state) corporation law in the United States, or under a European (as opposed to an English, Netherlands, etc.) corporation law in the European Union. With certain specialized exceptions (banks), there seems little likelihood of the United States moving to a system of federally chartered corporations. By contrast, many countries with federal systems (e.g., Germany) charter corporations under a national, rather than a local, corporate law. A few years ago, the European Council promulgated a regulation creating a "Societas Europaea" (an SE). The idea was to allow persons to form a European, rather than a German, English, etc. corporation. The SE, however, is a sort of mixing of national and European laws, such that an SE formed in one country will not follow all the same corporate rules as an SE formed in another country, and it is uncertain how much use this entity will see. *E.g.*, Theo Raaijmakers, *The Statute for a European Company: Its Impact on Board Structures, and Corporate Governance in the European Union*, 5 European Bus. Org. L. Rev. 1 (2004).

From a policy standpoint, what are the advantages the European Union seeks by harmonizing (or supplanting with an SE) national corporate laws? Are there some advantages the United States has gained by allowing different states to have different corporate laws? Will such divergence, when combined with free choice of corporate law, lead to ever less protective corporate law (a "race to the bottom"), or to ever more efficient corporate law ("a race to the top")?

3. The jurisdictional reach of United States securities laws is not limited to corporations formed or operating in the United States. Rather, the basis for jurisdiction under these laws is the use of means of interstate commerce, the United States mail, or a national securities exchange to engage in specified conduct (e.g., sale of a security). Hence, these laws apply to non-United States corporations that sell their stock in the United States, or, of particular significance, list their stock for trading on stock exchanges in the United States (such as the New York Stock Exchange).

The reach of United States securities laws to non-United States corporations based upon their listing stock or other securities for trading on the New York Stock Exchange creates its own prospects for choice of corporate law. Is it possible that some foreign corporations list on the New York Stock Exchange, less to have access to United States financial markets, than to subject themselves to United States securities laws? Why would a corporation wish to subject itself to potentially more burdensome regulation? Consider what unspoken message such an action might convey to potential investors in the corporation. For an empirical examination of whether Israeli corporations have been listing on United States stock exchanges in order to gain investor confidence by complying with higher United States disclosure requirements, see, *e.g.*, Ariel Yehezkel, *Foreign Corporations Listing in the United States—Does Law Matter? Testing the Israeli Phenomenon* (September 3, 2005), U Illinois Law & Economics Research Paper No. LE05–023, available at SSRN: http://ssrn.com/abstract=797504.

On the other hand, application of United States securities law to non-United States corporations, which list on the New York Stock Exchange, can create the sort of conflicts between inconsistent regulation that worried the court in *McDermott*. Section 301 of the Sarbanes–Oxley Act requires corporations, in order to list their stock on a national stock exchange in the United States, to have an audit committee of the board of directors, composed of independent directors, select the corporation's outside auditors. On its face, this creates conflicts with corporate statutes in some other jurisdictions in which either (i) shareholders select auditors, or (ii) employees are entitled to elect a certain percentage of the board (since the employee representatives might not meet the definition of an independent director for purposes of the Sarbanes–Oxley Act). One answer to such conflicts has been for the Securities Exchange Commission to create special rules for non-United States corporations. Securities Exchange Commission, Release Nos. 33–8220, 34–47654, Standards Relating to Listed Company Audit Committees, 68 FR

18788, 18802 (April 16, 2003). Another answer might be for foreign corporations to delist from United States stock exchanges. *E.g.*, Daniel Epstein, *Goodbye, Farewell, Auf Wiedersehen, Adieu* ... , Wall St. J. A10 (February 9, 2005).

4.   In discussing what corporate law governs a particular company, it is useful to note that the boundaries of what constitutes "corporate law" are not exact. Indeed, questions exist both as to what rules constitute "law" and what laws are part of "corporate" law.

For example, governmental and non-governmental organizations in many nations have adopted various corporate governance codes. *E.g.*, Robert A.G. Monks & Nell Minow, CORPORATE GOVERNANCE 251–258 (2d ed. 2001). These codes normally are voluntary in the sense that no legal liability results from the failure to comply—albeit, some national corporate laws may require companies publicly to explain failure to comply with the code, and various privileges (such as listing for trading on a stock exchange) may be denied for non-compliance. Many have argued that such codes create norms that impact corporate behavior even without sanctions attached. Hence, regardless of whether such codes are "law" (depending upon how one defines this term), corporate attorneys often find such codes of interest.

An earlier note referred to the 1933 Securities Act and 1934 Securities Exchange Act as national "corporate" law in the United States. Many readers might object by arguing that securities laws are not corporate law. In fact, many other nations include disclosure rules in their company laws, and so what is corporate law and what is capital markets (or securities) law is in the eye of the beholder. Similarly, some nations might have rules protecting creditors of corporations in the nation's corporate laws, while other nations might have rules along the same lines in bankruptcy or insolvency laws. Also, are laws giving workers a voice in running corporations part of corporate law or employment law? One impact of this divergence is to suggest that one should not decide which issues come within the internal affairs rule simply by rote application of the label corporate law. Another impact is to suggest that, in conducting legal research, especially involving law of another nation, the applicable rule could be in an entirely different body of law than one expected.

Chapter III

LIMITED LIABILITY AND CREDITOR PROTECTION

In the last two centuries, laws have spread throughout the world allowing the forms of business discussed in Chapter I, which insulate the owners' personal assets from obligations to pay the debts of the business. The traditional story is that the worldwide acceptance of these business forms reflects the utility, if not necessity, of limited liability for encouraging the aggregation of capital and the entrepreneurial efforts critical for achieving industrialization and economic prosperity. As the English magazine the *Economist* put it some eighty years ago:

> "The economic historian of the future may assign to the nameless inventor of the principle of limited liability, as applied to trading corporations, a place of honour with Watt and Stephenson, and other pioneers of the Industrial Revolution." *Economist* (December 18, 1926).

On the other hand, the skeptic might wonder how strange lands, like the state of California, were able to achieve industrialization and prosperity without providing limited liability to corporate stockholders until 1931. Be this as it may, limited liability for the owners of a business creates added risks for creditors of the business, which nations around the world have sought to mitigate through their corporate laws.

GEORGE ABU–NASSAR v. ELDERS FUTURES, INC.
1991 WL 45062 (S.D.N.Y. 1991).

Defendant Elders Futures Inc. ("Elders") has moved to compel plaintiffs George and Waleed Abu–Nassar (the "Abu–Nassars") to provide more complete answers to various interrogatories and document production requests relating to Elders' first, second and fifth counterclaims. Those counterclaims seek to hold the Abu–Nassars personally liable for the alleged indebtedness of Informative Investment Group, Ltd. ("Infovest"), a Lebanese corporation wholly owned by the Abu–Nassars. Besides opposing the discovery motion, the Abu–Nassars have cross-moved to dismiss these counterclaims, and the court is treating this motion as one for partial summary judgment. For the reasons that follow, the motion for partial summary judgment is denied and the motion to compel discovery is granted.

Statement of Facts.

This case is the result of the deteriorated relationship between Elders, a registered futures commission merchant incorporated in New York, and the Abu–Nassars, who are citizens of Lebanon and sole shareholders and principals of Infovest.[1] Infovest acted as an introducing broker[2] for commodities futures and options transactions and was organized as a limited liability company under Lebanese law.[3] In November 1983, Infovest entered into an agreement with Rudolf Wolff Commodity Brokers ("RWCB"), the predecessor of Elders, under which Infovest would solicit customers exclusively on behalf of RWCB and receive a share of the resulting commissions.[4] * * * The * * * Agreement provided, inter alia, that Infovest "guarantees the payment of all sums to RWCB in connection with or in any manner relating or resulting from the accounts, including, without limitation, margin calls and debit balances which may arise." This guarantee was originally secured by a $250,000 letter of credit of Infovest for the benefit of RWCB.

Various accounts were established at RWCB on behalf of Infovest and its principals. A portion of the commissions earned by Infovest was deposited in account 75001, to be used for Infovest's operating expenses in Beirut. Account 75002 was opened as a joint account for the three individual principals of Infovest (the Abu–Nassars and Gabriel Manougian, an employee of Infovest), and was to be used as the depository of the remainder of the commissions earned by Infovest. As of October 30, 1987, account 75002 had a balance of $49,825.17.

In March 1985, the Infovest letter of credit to RWCB was replaced by account 75003, into which George Abu–Nassar deposited $250,000 of his personal funds as security for the performance of Infovest's guarantee to RWCB. Elders permitted George Abu–Nassar to withdraw excess interest or earnings whenever the amount on deposit in this account exceeded the required $250,000. George Abu–Nassar deposited additional personal funds into account 75003, and they were invested, together with the original $250,000 security deposit, in United States Treasury Bills. As of October 30, 1987, account 75003 had a balance of $451,726.25. Finally, George Abu–Nassar opened account 75005 for his

---

1. George Abu–Nassar is president of Infovest, while his son Waleed is general manager.

2. An introducing broker has no direct ties to any markets, exchanges or boards of trade, but solicits customers to open accounts with another company, which executes the trades on behalf of the customers. The introducing broker earns commissions based on the transactions made by these customers.

3. A limited liability company "is a society without a firm name, constituted between a number of persons who subscribe with shares . . . and who are not liable for the debts of the company beyond the amounts of their contributions." Code of Commerce of Lebanon, Book II, Part III, Art. 77 (reprinted in XIV Commercial Laws of the World, Commercial Laws of Lebanon (1983 ed.)).

4. Elders succeeded to RWCB's business in July 1986.

personal commodities futures investments. This account contained $30,854.84 as of October 30, 1987.

On April 27, 1987, as a result of tremendous fluctuation in the price of silver futures contracts, a number of accounts at Elders for customers who had been introduced by Infovest sustained substantial deficits when their over-margined positions were liquidated. Elders covered the deficits, totalling $4,213,905.18, but the customers failed to deposit sufficient additional funds to balance their accounts. Infovest subsequently refused to pay the deficit when Elders requested that Infovest fulfill its guarantee obligations under the * * * Agreement. At the same time, Elders refused to remit the balance of accounts 75002, 75003 and 75005 to [the Abu–Nassars] and Infovest and froze the three accounts.

On November 23, 1987, Elders commenced a breach-of-contract action against Infovest in New York State Supreme Court, seeking payment of the deficits in the accounts of customers introduced by Infovest. On February 18, 1988, Infovest filed an answer and counterclaim, which sought the withheld commissions and the funds in the various accounts at Elders, as well as over twenty million dollars in compensatory and punitive damages.

The present federal action was commenced by the Abu–Nassars on November 7, 1988, seeking damages under section 4(b) of the Commodity Exchange Act, as well as section 10(b) of the Securities Exchange Act of 1934, and Rule 10b–5 of the Securities and Exchange Commission. [The Abu–Nassars] also assert common law claims of conversion and breach of contract with respect to the funds held in accounts 75002, 75003 and 75005.

In its answer and counterclaims, Elders contends that the Abu–Nassars are the alter ego of Infovest, and that as a result they are personally liable for the deficits in the accounts of those customers introduced by Infovest. * * *

The parties have undertaken substantial discovery in both the state and the federal actions, including a lengthy August 1989 deposition of the Abu–Nassars in London. Nonetheless, they have encountered a roadblock based on their divergent views as to the merits of Elders' effort to impose personal liability on the Abu–Nassars for the debts of Infovest. The specific source of contention is Elders' First Set of Interrogatories and a supplemental document request, which were served on November 3, 1989. * * * Although the Abu–Nassars answered some of the questions, they refused to answer any questions relating to Elders' attempt to pierce the corporate veil of Infovest, arguing primarily that Elders had failed to make a preliminary showing with respect to its alter ego claim and that it was therefore not entitled to any discovery on that allegation.

* * *

On April 24, 1990, [Elders] moved to compel [the Abu–Nassars] to provide more complete answers to its interrogatories and document production requests. On May 16, 1990 [the Abu–Nassars] responded with a motion to dismiss Elders' first, second and fifth counterclaims, which incorporate allegations that Infovest was the alter ego of [the Abu–Nassars] and that [the Abu–Nassars] fraudulently stripped Infovest of its assets to avoid paying their obligations to Elders. The court converted [the Abu–Nassars] motion into one for partial summary judgment, and the parties were given the opportunity to supplement the evidentiary record.

ANALYSIS

I. Summary Judgment

* * *

B. Choice of Law

The first issue we face is the choice of law governing a suit in an American court attacking the corporate status of a foreign corporation. This question is relevant to both the substantive law governing requirements of corporate form and the applicable standards for piercing the corporate veil. This court looks to foreign law regarding requirements of corporate status for a foreign corporation, but with respect to piercing the corporate veil of a foreign corporation, different choice of law principles may be applicable. See *Itel Containers Int'l Corp. v. Atlanttrafik Express Serv. Ltd.*, 1988 WL 75262 (S.D.N.Y. July 13, 1988) ("As a general matter, the law of the state of incorporation normally determines issues relating to the internal affairs of a corporation.... Different conflicts principles, however, apply where the rights of third parties external to the corporation are at issue.").

Elders asserts that New York law is controlling on all issues, since the * * * Agreement between Elders and Infovest stated that New York law would govern "this agreement and all matters relating hereto." [The Abu–Nassars] counter that the "governing law" provision in the * * * Agreement applies only to issues of interpretation regarding the rights and obligations of the parties under the agreement and does not cover issues of corporate status. [The Abu–Nassars] contend that since Infovest was organized as a Lebanese limited liability company, Lebanese law should govern issues of corporate organization and alter ego liability.

There is no need to resolve this issue at this stage, however, since partial summary judgment is not appropriate under either Lebanese or New York law. * * *

c [*sic*]. Lebanese Law

Under Lebanese law, shareholders of a limited liability company are generally not liable for any obligations of the company above their initial capital contributions. (See Lebanese Code, Title VII, Book II, Art. 1.) There are, however, certain statutory requirements that must be satisfied for the company to qualify as a limited liability company. Among others, the name of the company must reflect its object or the adoption of a "style" comprising the name of one or more of its partners (id., Art.

6); the object or purpose of the company must not fall into one of several prohibited categories, including "capital investment operations for the account of Third Parties"[9] (id., Art. 4); the capitalization must exceed 50,000 Lebanese pounds (id., Art. 7); the phrase "limited liability company" and the amount of the company's capital "are to figure prominently on all printed matter, advertisements, publications and other documents emanating from the company" (id., Art. 6); and the company must hold an annual meeting to review the company's business affairs prior to the declaration or distribution of profits. (Id., Art. 21.) Finally, Article 12 provides that "any limited liability company is void and of no effect among its partners when formed in violation of the conditions required in the preceding articles." Moreover, "when nullity of the company is pronounced [under these provisions], the partners who have been the cause of nullity ... are jointly responsible to Third Parties ... for the damage resulting from such nullity." (Id., Art. 13.)

[Elders]   appear[s] to contend that Infovest failed to comply with Articles 4, 6, 7 and 21, and that therefore its limited liability status may be set aside under Article 13 and personal liability imposed on the Abu–Nassars.

* * *

In accordance with Article 6 of the Lebanese Code, the full name of Infovest, Informative Investment Group, Ltd., unquestionably reflects the company's object. What is less clear is whether Infovest's activities as an introducing broker were permissible under Article 4 of the Lebanese Code.

* * *

As noted, the Lebanese Code also requires a minimum capitalization of 50,000 Lebanese pounds. Infovest's original capitalization was 200,000 Lebanese pounds, and was significantly in excess of that figure through 1986. Nonetheless, [the Abu–Nassars] admit that since at least July 1987, Infovest's liabilities have exceeded its assets, Infovest has been required to borrow funds from [the Abu–Nassars] in order to pay its obligations, and George Abu–Nassar has personally paid certain debts of the company. Although the Lebanese legal experts do not address whether these factors constitute undercapitalization and what the consequences might be, I note that if Infovest has in fact been undercapitalized since July 1987, Article 7 of the Lebanese Code provides an opportunity for a company to recapitalize within one year before any negative consequences could be imposed.[11] In the present case, more than three and one-half years has elapsed since July 1987, and [the Abu–Nassars] have not only failed to recapitalize Infovest, but it appears that

9. The parties' Lebanese law experts apparently translate Article 4 differently, but this does not alter the analysis. * * *

11. The negative consequences include transforming the limited liability company into another corporate form in which the individual shareholders could be liable, or allowing any rightful claimant to petition for the dissolution of the company. (See Lebanese Code, Art. 7.)

the company is essentially out of business. Thus, if Infovest is in fact undercapitalized, it appears that under Article 7 [the Abu–Nassars] may be exposed to personal liability based on this undercapitalization. As a result of unresolved issues as to Infovest's capitalization and the implications of a possible undercapitalization, there are material issues of fact concerning whether Infovest was in compliance at the relevant time with Article 7 of the Code.

The Lebanese Code also requires that "immediately after the name of the company the following phrase: 'limited liability company' and the amount of its capital are to figure prominently on all printed matter . . . emanating from the company." It is clear that the Infovest letterhead did not state its capitalization or use the required phrase, but rather used the term "Ltd." The parties agree that the abbreviation "Ltd." is a permissible alternative to the required language. Elders' expert contends, however, that the statement of capitalization is an important warning to third parties as to the limited liability of the partners. Without such a statement, there may be a presumption of deceit by the company, which could lead to the personal liability of the partners if a third party were induced into a transaction based on a violation of this provision. * * *

[The Abu–Nassars'] expert * * * claims that shareholders in a limited liability company cannot be held personally liable to third parties if the company states explicitly that it is a limited liability company, as Infovest clearly did. * * * Thus, there is an open question under Lebanese law as to whether failure to state the company's capitalization leads to a presumption of deceit, what evidence could be introduced by [the Abu–Nassars] to rebut the presumption, and the effect of including "Ltd." in the company's title. Furthermore, there is an open factual question as to whether [the Abu–Nassars'] failure to state Infovest's capitalization in any way deceived Elders as to Infovest's nature and capitalization.

Finally, the Lebanese Code requires that a limited liability company hold an annual meeting prior to declaring and distributing profits. In the present case, [the Abu–Nassars] admit that no formal annual meetings were held, but rather state that meetings were "informal and not recorded, as is permitted by Lebanese law." [The Abu–Nassars'] legal expert asserts that shareholders of a limited liability company may receive "interim dividends" before an annual shareholder meeting. While [Elder's] expert does not address the viability of "interim dividends" under Lebanese law, he stresses that failure to comply with the shareholder meeting requirement before distributing profits based on an accurate balance sheet subjects the managers of the company to personal liability for "swindling." Both Lebanese authorities agree that any improper dividends must be returned to the corporation.

In the present case, it is uncontroverted that money earned as commissions was deposited by Elders in account 75002 for the personal benefit of [the Abu–Nassars] and Gabriel Manougian. [Elders] claims that this money constituted corporate profits of Infovest that were deposited into a personal account of the company's shareholders without proper authorization from the shareholders of the company. [The Abu–Nassars] contend, on the other hand, that such deposits constituted the payment of salaries, repayment of advances or the withdrawal of profits. Irrespective of the proper interpretation of Lebanese law regarding "interim dividends," there remains a material factual question as to whether the amounts deposited into account 75002 were properly authorized salary payments or dividends, as opposed to payments of profits directly to the personal account of [the Abu–Nassars] in contravention of Lebanese law. As noted, to the extent that any portions of these payments were improper dividends, the Abu–Nassars would be personally liable for the repayment of those funds to Infovest.

The foregoing adequately demonstrates the existence of genuine disputes with respect to material facts concerning Infovest's alleged non-compliance with the Lebanese Code. The record is somewhat less clear concerning the consequence of such non-compliance.

Article 12 provides for a declaration of nullity for a limited liability company based on non-compliance with the cited Code sections, but it expressly limits its effect to relations between partners. Article 13 seems more pertinent. It provides:

> When nullity of the company is pronounced in pursuance of the provisions of the preceding article, the partners who have been the cause of nullity, the initial Managers and Founders are jointly responsible to Third Parties as they are to the other partners for the damages resulting from such nullity.

* * *

The complication in this matter is introduced by the apparent requirement that the party seeking the nullification must have been injured by the company's violation of the Code, a requirement implicit in the language of Article 13 * * *. Moreover, other substantive Code provisions also incorporate such a causation requirement. Thus, Article 6, which requires a notation of the company's limited liability status and the extent of its capitalization, goes on to provide, in Mr. Saade's [an expert witness] translation:

> Any infringement of the preceding dispositions is punished with a penalty of one thousand to three thousand pounds. If this infringement has deceived third parties as to the nature of the company, then the dispositions ruling the partnership[] may apply in order to determine the liability of the partners.

In other words, the company would lose its limited liability status if its failure to include the required notations actually deceived a third-party into believing that it was dealing with a partnership, and hence could hold the individual partners liable.

It is not at all clear on the current record whether [Elders was] injured by any of the alleged violations of the Code. For example, since

Infovest used the term "Ltd.," it is doubtful that Elders could claim to have been deceived into believing that Infovest was not purporting to be a limited liability company. It is also not at all obvious that [Elders] was injured by the asserted failure of Infovest to hold required shareholder meetings, and in any event, it appears that such a failure would not provide a basis for holding the shareholders directly liable to third parties for obligations of the company. * * *

Notwithstanding these doubts, summary judgment cannot be entered in favor of [the Abu–Nassars] insofar as Lebanese law may be applicable. First, Elders may well have standing to press for nullification based on Infovest's alleged undercapitalization, since this condition may have prevented Elders from obtaining compensation from Infovest to which it is allegedly entitled under the guarantee provisions of the Agency Agreement. Second, although not entirely clear, Infovest may have been acting as an investment manager for its clients in possible violation of the Code, and that violation by itself could be viewed as contributing to the injury allegedly suffered by Elders. Third, the manager may be liable for corporate debts if he authorized dividend payments to shareholders without an accurate balance sheet. (See Lebanese Code, Art. 35) Fourth, in any event Infovest has not, by its summary judgment motion, put into issue the question of whether Infovest's alleged violations of the Lebanese Code caused injury to Elders. Accordingly, Elders has not been called upon on this motion to establish causation, and cannot be denied the opportunity to do so at an appropriate time.

C [sic]. New York Law

Even if Infovest's corporate form were preserved under the laws governing Lebanese limited liability companies, the Abu–Nassars could be held personally liable if the corporate veil were pierced under New York law. As a general rule, courts are reluctant to disregard the corporate entity, * * *.

Nonetheless, the corporate form may be pierced "when it can be demonstrated that the [corporate] form has been used to achieve fraud, or when the corporation has been so dominated by an individual ... and its separate identity so disregarded, that it primarily transacted the dominator's business rather than its own and can be called the other's alter ego."

The courts have identified a number of factors that must be considered in deciding whether to pierce the corporate veil, including (1) intermingling of personal and corporate funds and siphoning of corporate funds by a principal; (2) failure to observe corporate formalities and keep proper books and records; (3) failure to pay dividends; (4) inadequate capitalization; (5) insolvency; and (6) perpetuation of fraud by shareholders in maintaining the corporate form.

* * *[T]his list of factors is not exhaustive, and * * * as a general rule alter ego liability would be imposed "when doing so would achieve an equitable result." *William Wrigley Jr. Co. v. Waters*, 890 F.2d at 601. While noting the "literally infinite variety of situations which might

warrant a court to pierce the corporate veil," the *Wrigley* panel cautioned that

> "preoccupation with questions of structure, financial and accounting sophistication or dividend policy or history would inevitably beckon the end of limited liability for small business owners, many, if not most, of whom have chosen the corporate form to shield themselves from unlimited liability and potential financial ruin."

However, the court in *Wrigley* also commented that piercing the corporate veil had been justified upon proof of an abuse of the corporate form "either through on-going fraudulent activities of a principal, or a pronounced and intimate commingling of the corporation and its principal or principals, which prompted the reviewing courts, driven by equity, to disregard the corporate form." For example, in *Dow Chemical Pacific Ltd. v. Rascator Maritime S.A.*, 782 F.2d at 343, the corporate veil was pierced where the corporation had no employees or records of meetings, stock, or elected directors and had only one individual with authority to sign checks, and where funds were shuffled between personal and corporate accounts.

In the present case, the Abu–Nassars are the sole shareholders and principal officers of Infovest. Clearly, the simple fact that they oversaw and controlled the ... business does not mean that the corporate entities were mere alter egos. * * * An examination of the various veil-piercing factors, however, indicates that summary judgment on Elders' counterclaims for alter ego liability is inappropriate, as there are a number of genuine disputes of material fact, the resolution of which may ultimately justify piercing Infovest's corporate veil.

[Elder's] attempt to demonstrate that [the Abu–Nassars] dominated Infovest and abused its corporate form rests largely on allegations that the Abu–Nassars intermingled personal and corporate funds and siphoned corporate funds for their personal use, "without regard to formality and to suit their individual convenience." This claim receives at least some support from the undisputed fact that profits and commissions earned by Infovest were deposited directly into account 75002, a joint personal account of [the Abu–Nassars] and Gabriel Manougian, an employee of Infovest.

Elders also argues that George Abu–Nassar's use of personal funds to replace the $250,000 Infovest letter of credit, and his deposit of additional personal funds in the same account, to be invested with the existing funds in the account, also demonstrates an intermingling of personal and corporate funds. Additionally, Elders alleges that there was an oral agreement between the Abu–Nassars and Elders in May or June of 1987, in which the Abu–Nassars agreed to forego their monthly commissions in order to pay off the deficits in the customer accounts. Finally, Elders points to the fact that the Abu–Nassars admitted that George Abu–Nassar paid about $100,000 out of his own funds to satisfy Infovest debts to other Lebanese brokers, in order to protect his business reputation, and that loans were made by the Abu–Nassars to Infovest to allow it to pay its expenses.

Not surprisingly, the Abu–Nassars contest each of these arguments. They assert that as a result of the unstable political conditions existing in Lebanon at the time, they undertook to deposit corporate funds in their personal accounts to allow Infovest to channel payments to them for salary, commissions, expense reimbursements and profits without exposing the funds to possible seizure in Beirut.

This factual dispute cannot be resolved by summary judgment. Although most, if not all, of the transfers to [the Abu–Nassars'] personal accounts and the personal payments and loans of George Abu–Nassar to satisfy Infovest's corporate obligations may have been properly authorized and entirely legitimate, [Elders] has come forward with sufficient evidence to raise a material factual issue as to whether there was intermingling or siphoning of funds by the Abu–Nassars, and whether this constituted sufficient domination of the corporate form by [the Abu–Nassars] to justify piercing the corporate veil.

Other factors in this case also lead to the conclusion that summary judgment is not appropriate at this time with respect to Elder's alter ego claim. First, there are a number of unresolved issues with respect to the observance of corporate formalities.[17] For example, it is not clear whether Infovest maintained proper books and records. Although the Abu–Nassars claim that such records exist and are in the custody of Waleed Abu–Nassar, and that they include both customer account records and financial and accounting records, those books and records have not been turned over to defendant as a result of [the Abu–Nassars'] objection to the interrogatory and document production requests seeking such information. Accordingly, there is no way to determine the sufficiency of the purported corporate records. * * *

With respect to dividends, Infovest has never held an official annual meeting and has therefore had no opportunity to declare dividends. Although it could perhaps be argued that the money in account 75002 constituted interim dividends, [the Abu–Nassars] have not differentiated between monies paid as salaries and company earnings paid to the individual shareholders of Infovest. Moreover, to the extent that any such "interim dividends" were not directly supported by earnings, Lebanese law requires that such payments be returned to the company. The failure of Infovest ever to declare a dividend to its shareholders lends additional credence to Elders' theory of alter ego liability and further supports denial of the motion for partial summary judgment.

Infovest's alleged undercapitalization and insolvency further support denial of [the Abu–Nassars'] motion for partial summary judgment. "Although undercapitalization alone is not a sufficient ground for disregarding the corporate veil, it nevertheless is an additional factor to be weighed in the balance. However, the mere fact that an entity may or

17. When determining whether a foreign corporation has observed the proper corporate formalities, courts apply the law of the country of incorporation.

may not have the capital to respond to a potential large award against it does not justify piercing the corporate veil." This court measures undercapitalization in terms of the size of the corporate undertaking, and will deem a corporation undercapitalized if it is "wholly reliant on [an individual] for the operating funds necessary for its continuing existence. . . . " The Abu–Nassars admit that since at least July 1987, Infovest's liabilities have exceeded its assets, and [the Abu–Nassars] have loaned personal assets to Infovest to meet its operating expenses.

These circumstances indicate that, notwithstanding the balances in the disputed frozen accounts at Elders, Infovest is currently undercapitalized and essentially insolvent, in that its liabilities exceed its assets, it is no longer in business and it can no longer meet its obligations without financial assistance from [the Abu–Nassars]. * * *

Finally, there is at least a potentially colorable claim that [the Abu–Nassars'] conduct vis-a-vis Infovest may have involved an element of fraud. This claim is premised on the Abu–Nassars' alleged failure to state the extent of Infovest's capitalization on all its documents, as purportedly required by Lebanese law; Infovest's undercapitalization and [the Abu–Nassars'] payment of certain corporate obligations; the admitted perpetuation of Infovest's corporate existence merely to litigate against Elders; and the alleged fraudulent transfer of Infovest's assets to a similar corporate entity controlled by [the Abu–Nassars] in an effort to render Infovest an empty shell and thereby defraud Infovest's creditors.

* * *

Accordingly, [the Abu–Nassars'] motion for partial summary judgment on [Elders'] first, second and fifth counterclaims is denied.

* * *

Notes

1.   What law should govern this case? Are the limits on limited liability an "internal affair" so that the law of the state or nation of formation should govern? Review the reaction of the European Court of Justice in the *Inspire Art* decision in Chapter II to the argument that the host country has an interest in safeguarding its creditors. In any event, if New York law should apply, why does the court treat a Lebanese limited liability company as a "corporation" for purposes of New York law? If Lebanese law applies, what difficulty did the court have in determining the law of Lebanon? Finally, why was the applicable "law" not simply the contract the parties made—which provided the creditor with protection (albeit inadequate in hindsight) against the risks of limited liability?

2.   The refusal of the court in *Abu–Nassar* to decide whether New York or Lebanese law would govern the case creates a nice opportunity to compare approaches taken by corporate laws in the United States versus other nations to protect creditors from excessive risks due to limited liability. These approaches fall into a number of categories:

(i) *Disclosure*

One protection corporate law may provide for creditors is mandatory disclosure by the borrowing company regarding its status and finances. The rationale is that such disclosure better enables prospective creditors to protect themselves in deciding whether to do business with a firm whose owners enjoy limited liability. *Abu–Nassar* illustrates that there are differences between the law in the United States versus laws often found outside the United States with respect to such disclosure.

State corporations statutes in the United States typically include only one requirement for disclosure to prospective creditors: The company's name must contain a term, such as "Corporation," "corp.," "Company," "Co.," "Incorporated," or "Inc.," that signifies the company is in a form whose owners enjoy limited liability. Beyond this, the vast majority of corporations in the United States, which have not sold stocks or bonds to the general public, typically face no statutory requirement to disclose their finances to prospective creditors or to the public generally.

Corporate laws outside the United States also typically require that the name of the company contain a term identifying the form of business—such as the recognizable "Ltd" found in the name of the Lebanese company in *Abu–Nassar*, or the less familiar "GmbH" or "AG" found in the names of German private or marketable stock companies. *E.g.*, Gesetz betreffend die GmbH [Company with Limited Liability Act] § 4; Aktiengesetz [Stock Company Act] § 4. In contrast to corporate laws in the United States, however, corporate laws in other nations often go further and demand financial disclosure to prospective creditors or to the public by businesses, even if not publicly held, so long as the business is in a form providing limited liability. The Lebanese statute involved in *Abu–Nassar* contained a rather crude financial disclosure requirement in mandating that the company's correspondence set forth the company's "capital." More broadly, laws in the European Union require all companies to file for public inspection financial statements prepared in accordance with minimum accounting standards. *E.g., First Council Directive*, 68/151, 1968 O.J. (L 65/8) 41 (EC) (the company laws of all member nations in the European Union must require that companies file for public inspection annual balance sheets, income statements, and statements as to the amount of the companies' subscribed capital); *Fourth Council Directive*, 78/660, 1978 O.J. (L 222) 11 (EC) (containing various accounting requirements that member nations are to impose for the preparation of financial statements mandated under the First Directive; albeit with exemptions allowing member nations to relax the accounting rules for smaller companies).

Just how significant is this difference in creditor protection between the United States as compared with nations whose laws mandate financial disclosure by private companies to prospective creditors? In the absence of mandatory public disclosure, might prospective creditors in the United States protect themselves by demanding financial statements from the corporation, or by getting a report from a credit rating service, before agreeing to do business with the corporation? Consider also the role that enforcement practices (or the lack thereof) could play in producing convergence between regimes with nominally different statutory requirements. For example, in Germany (which had been hesitant to impose reporting requirements on its private companies (GmbH)), the vast majority of private companies might not be providing the required financial disclosure. *E.g.,* Case C–191/95 EC Commission v. Federal Republic of Germany, 1998 E.C.R. I–5449 (the European Commission found 93 percent non-compliance with annual financial reporting requirements by German companies up to 1990).

In *Abu–Nassar*, the court believed that non-compliance with disclosure requirements did not create liability toward a creditor under Lebanese law unless the creditor could prove deceit. If, however, non-compliance with mandatory disclosure only creates liability in the event the non-compliance deceives the creditor, then we may have arrived at the point in which corporate laws within and outside the United States show a substantial similarity regarding disclosure to creditors of non-public corporations. Recall that one of the grounds listed by the court in *Abu–Nassar* for piercing the corporate veil under New York law was fraud. Fraud is also a frequently accepted ground for imposing liability upon a company's controlling owners for the company's debts under the laws of other nations. *E.g.,* Juan M. Dobson, *Lifting the Veil in Four Countries: The Law of Argentina, England, France and the United States*, 35 Int'l & Comp. L.Q. 839, 840–47 (1986). Notice the rather expansive way in which the court seemed to treat the concept of fraud under New York law in *Abu–Nassar*. For example, the court listed as possible fraud the use of the owner's personal funds to pay corporate bills (which can provide the corporation a better credit record than justified by the company's financial situation). Could a broad concept of fraud provide the basis for penalizing non-disclosure of perhaps the most important fact to a creditor dealing with a private corporation—this being the controlling owner's knowledge, at the time his or her company incurs the debt, that the company will be unable to pay this bill?

(ii) *Initial Capitalization Requirements*

Another protection corporate law may provide for creditors involves the required initial capitalization of the company. The notion is that forcing the corporation's owners to provide some capital decreases the risk faced by the corporation's creditors, both by establishing a cushion to absorb losses and by giving the owners better incentives for responsible management. *Abu–Nassar* also illustrates that there are differences in the laws governing required initial capitalization in the United States, as compared with the corporate laws in many other nations.

Perhaps the simplest initial capital requirement is in statutes that require the owners of a corporation to pay into the company at least an amount specified in the statute prior to the company initiating its business. At one time, such provisions were common in the United States, with statutes often setting the minimum capital at $1000. These provisions have virtually disappeared from the United States. As illustrated by the Lebanese statute in *Abu–Nassar*, the same is not true outside the United States, where statutes setting out the minimum amount of paid in capital a company must have before beginning business remain common. *E.g., Second Council Directive*, 77/91, 1976 O.J. (L 26/1) 1 (EC) (the company laws of member nations in the European Union must require a minimum capital of at least 25,000 euros for marketable stock companies); Marcus Lutter, *Limited*

Liability Companies and Private Companies, in XIII INTERNATIONAL ENCYCLOPEDIA OF COMPARATIVE LAW 9 (1998) (containing a list of minimum capital requirements as of 1996 in 40 nations other than the United States, showing that 31 impose such a requirement).

A more complicated set of legal requirements regarding a corporation's capital are those governing what the corporation must receive when selling its stock. In the United States, directors have more leeway in this area than is the case in many other countries. For example, directors in the United States have no obligation to ensure that the corporation sell any particular amount of stock. By contrast, corporate laws in civil law countries often require that the company receive subscriptions (promises to purchase its stock) for the entire amount of capital designated in the company's articles, and that all, or at least a designated fraction, of the subscriptions must be fully paid prior to the company commencing business. *E.g.*, Gesetz betreffend die GmbH §§ 5(3), 7(2); Aktiengesetz § 23(2), (3). Moreover, in the United States, the directors' judgment as to the value of any non-cash consideration received by the corporation for its stock typically is conclusive in the absence of fraud. By contrast, laws in European countries often require third party verification that the value of any non-cash consideration received by a company for its stock equals what the directors specified. *E.g.*, *Second Council Directive, supra* at art. 10 (the company laws of member nations in the European Union must require that marketable stock companies, which receive non-cash consideration for their stock, publish a report, prepared by one or more independent experts appointed or approved by an administrative or judicial authority, that describes the assets and the methods of their valuation); Gesetz betreffend die GmbH § 9c (the court shall refuse to register a German private company, thereby not bringing the company into official existence, if the court finds that contributions in kind are overvalued).

A final form of initial capital requirement is for a court to determine the adequacy of the corporation's initial capitalization for the risks of the corporation's particular business. *Abu–Nassar* shows how courts in the United States might pierce the corporate veil and hold the owner(s) personally liable for the company's debts based upon a variety of factors, one of which is a finding of "inadequate capitalization" (which is usually, unlike the approach of the court in *Abu–Nassar*, evaluated based upon the corporation's capitalization at the inception of the business, and, in any event, is not well defined). The court in *Abu–Nassar* never discusses whether Lebanese law provides for a similar remedy based upon a judicial evaluation of whether the company had inadequate capitalization. In fact, laws in other nations are mixed as to whether judicially determined inadequate capitalization provides grounds for piercing the corporate veil. *E.g.*, Carston Alting, *Piercing The Corporate Veil in American and German Law—Liability of Individuals and Entities: A Comparative View*, 2 Tulsa J. Comp. & Int'l L. 187, 208–209 (1995) (German cases are inconclusive as to whether a court will piece the corporate veil based upon a judicial finding of inadequate capitalization); Lutter, *supra*, at 35 (after a Belgium court rejected piercing the corporate veil for inadequate capitalization, the legislature responded by revising article 229 of Belgium's private company law to impose liability upon the company's founders for the company's debts if the company fails within three years because of manifest capital insufficiency).

Why did statutory minimum capital requirements die out in the United States, but remain popular abroad? Why are some courts in other countries unwilling to pierce the corporate veil based upon a judicial determination that the company had inadequate capitalization for the risks of the business? Is there some advantage to a simple capital requirement set by statute and known to all companies in advance? What is its disadvantage? Is there some advantage to a judicial evaluation of adequate capital tailored to the facts involving a particular business? What is its disadvantage? Regardless of whether the initial capitalization requirement comes from a statute setting a specific sum, or from a judicial evaluation of the company's capitalization, why should the adequacy of a company's capital not be a matter for creditors to assess for themselves before agreeing to deal with the corporation? Are there some differences the law should draw in this regard between different types of creditors? Do either the statutory or judicial approaches to required minimum capitalization draw such a distinction? Notice a difference between the statutory and judicially imposed minimum or adequate capitalization rules and the rules regarding consideration the corporation must receive for its stock. Do the rules in many European countries requiring full subscription of the capital set out in the articles, and an independent evaluation of the worth of non-cash consideration, attempt to dictate a minimum acceptable capitalization; or do they simply require the company to say in its articles what it will receive for its stock and to live up to that commitment in valuing non-cash consideration? In other words, might these rules really be about disclosing rather than dictating the corporation's capital? Finally, why does the law in many nations focus on the corporation's initial capital, when such capital probably will have been long gone before the company fails?

(iii) *Continuing Capitalization Requirements—Dealing with Losses*

Rather than just focus on the corporation's initial capitalization, corporate law could seek to protect creditors by requiring the corporation to maintain a level of capital. We shall return shortly to the topic of maintaining corporate capital by curbing the stockholders' withdrawal of assets from the company. Suppose, however, business losses wipe out the company's capital. At first glance, requiring the stockholders to replace capital in the face of continuing losses would seem at war with the whole notion of limited liability—indeed, this is why courts in the United States usually measure inadequate capitalization based upon capital at the inception of the business, rather than at the company's demise. Yet, this presumes the choice is between limited liability and a rule that would obligate the stockholders to pour money continuously into a business black hole. Laws outside the United States suggest another possible alternative.

As illustrated by the Lebanese statute discussed in *Abu–Nassar*, laws in a number of nations impose an obligation upon those in control of a corporation either to recapitalize or to liquidate a company when losses cause the company's capital to dip below a certain point. *E.g.*, Code de commerce art. L. 225–248 (under the French Commercial Code, a company must dissolve if it experiences losses that reduce stockholders' equity below half of the subscribed capital, unless the company reduces its stated capital correspondingly within two financial years and the resulting capital is higher than the statutory minimum capital); Codice civile artt. 2447, 2448(4) (under the Italian Civil Code, a company must dissolve if it experiences losses which reduce the stockholders' equity below the statutory minimum level of capital, unless the company recapitalizes or converts into another kind of company with a lesser capital requirement). More broadly, most nations other than the United States require corporate directors to have the company file bankruptcy as soon as the company becomes insolvent—which, in some nations, includes having less assets than debts (in other words, stockholder equity has gone below zero). *E.g.*, Aktiengesetz § 92; Gesetz betreffend die GmbH § 64.

What is the reason for requiring owners of a corporation, which is incurring losses that have chewed up the owners' equity in the company, to put in more of their own money or call it quits, rather than continuing to run the company on borrowed money? Consider the incentive limited liability creates in a situation in which a corporation is incurring losses financed entirely by borrowed money. What protection do creditors in the United States have against such a risk in the absence of a recapitalize or liquidate rule? In any event, is there some downside to forcing the liquidation of businesses that might be able to turn around? Of course, countries with a recapitalize or liquidate rule still have corporations that end up being unable to pay all of their debts in bankruptcy. To the extent this happens because those in control of the corporation did not realize in time the sorry state of the company's assets versus its debts, what does this say about the utility of a recapitalize or liquidate rule? To this extent this happens because, as in Lebanon, the law allows a considerable period of time before those in control of the company must act, does this undermine the whole point? To the extent this happens because those in control of the corporation realize the state of the company's assets versus its debts, but, as apparently the case in *Abu–Nassar*, continue anyway in disregard of their obligations, what should be the consequences?

Other than a mechanical continuing capital maintenance requirement, is there a way in which laws in the United States or other nations can create incentives for those in charge of a corporation to wrap it up in the face of continuing losses, or otherwise to take into account creditor interests when the company is operating on borrowed money? Consider the English law of "wrongful trading." Section 214 of the English Insolvency Act of 1986 empowers English courts to hold directors of a company in liquidation personally liable when the directors knew or should have known before commencing liquidation that there was no reasonable prospect that the company could have avoided liquidation, but failed to take every reasonable step to minimize the potential loss to the company's creditors. More broadly, consider whether a corporation's directors' should have a duty of care or loyalty toward the corporation's creditors—a subject to which this book will return when considering mismanagement by directors and controlling stockholders in Chapter V. To what extent can piercing the corporate veil in the United States achieve the same effect? For example, consider whether the controlling shareholder commits fraud if he or she continues to have the corporation incur new obligations once he or she knows the corporation will be unable to pay those bills.

(iv) *Curbing Asset Withdrawals by Stockholders*

Every jurisdiction recognizes the need to prevent a corporation's owners from abusing limited liability by taking the company's assets for the owners themselves and leaving the company's creditors high and dry. *Abu–Nassar* illustrates, not surprisingly, that there are differences between the laws in the United States, versus in other countries, to prevent abusive withdrawal of assets by a corporation's owners.

Corporation statutes in the United States and in other countries limit distributions from a corporation to its stockholders, whether through dividends or repurchases of stock. A difference exists, however, between corporate laws in most of the United States versus corporate laws in many other nations when it comes to the measure of a permissible dividend or other distribution to stockholders. In almost every state in the United States, except California, corporate statutes allow a corporation to pay dividends or to repurchase its stock until the company reaches the cusp of insolvency—in other words, the remaining assets just equal the company's debts. (This takes a little finagling under traditional statutes such as Delaware's, but is now explicit in the Model Business Corporation Act.) By contrast, laws in European nations normally prohibit dividends and share repurchases that would return to the stockholders what the stockholders paid in as subscribed capital, and, instead, limit dividends to paying out accumulated profits (or even just accumulated profits less a reserve). Moreover, even when allowing a distribution following a voluntary reduction in subscribed capital, corporate laws in European nations, unlike corporate laws in the United States, often create protections to substitute for the withdrawn capital cushion. *E.g.,* *Second Council Directive, supra* at art. 15, 32 (the company laws of member nations in the European Union must prohibit marketable stock companies from paying dividends or other distributions to their stockholders that would leave assets less than liabilities plus subscribed capital, and must prohibit distributions following a voluntary reduction in subscribed capital unless existing creditors receive security for their claims); Aktiengesetz §§ 57, 150, 225 (similar rules, except also mandating that companies set aside a certain proportion of profits in reserve, for German marketable stock companies); Gesetz betreffend die GmbH §§ 29, 30, 33, 58 (similar, but without mandatory reserves, for German private companies). (Incidentally, the dividend procedure called for by the Lebanese statute discussed in *Abu–Nassar*— having the annual stockholders meeting declare and distribute profits, rather than, as in the United States, leaving the determination of dividend distributions to the directors to undertake when and as the directors deem fit—generally follows the German approach. Aktiengesetz §§ 174–175.)

What protection do creditors of corporations in the United States have against dividends and stock repurchases that would strip the corporation of all capital cushion (particularly if creditors had relied upon such a cushion in deciding to transact business with the corporation)? Does the lack of such protection in corporate statutes in the United States explain the prevalence of dividend and share repurchase restrictions found in major lending contracts entered with corporations in the United States? Is there some advantage to leaving this issue to individually negotiated contracts? Are there some creditors who will not be a position to negotiate for such protection?

Can such creditors free-ride on the restrictions negotiated by other creditors?

As illustrated by *Abu–Nassar*, the problem of stockholders taking corporate assets in the closely held company often does not involve excessive dividends or repurchases of stock. Instead, it involves the sort of informal mixing of company and personal assets, use of company assets for personal benefit, or mixing of assets between different business entities under common ownership, that one might expect of a business person who views the business literally as his or hers—coupled perhaps, as seen in *Abu–Nassar*, with an after-the-fact effort to characterize the withdrawals as representing the payment of a salary or the like. In this situation, corporate laws in the United States and in other nations converge around a couple of approaches. One rather universal approach, mentioned by the court in *Abu–Nassar* as part of its application of Lebanese law, would be to require the owner to return sums found to be paid or received in violation his or her duty to the corporation. The other approach, applied under New York law by the court in *Abu–Nassar*, is to pierce the corporate veil and hold the owner liable for the corporation's debts (which could be more than the owner inappropriately took out of the corporation). There seems to be a similar willingness by courts in many other nations to lift the corporate veil and impose personal liability on the offending owner for the corporation's debts. *E.g.*, Lutter, *supra* at 102; Dobson, *supra* at 856–57, 859–861; J. Mark Ramseyer & Minoru Nakazato, JAPANESE LAW: AN ECONOMIC APPROACH 117–118 (1999).

The broad condemnation of corporate owners who take corporate assets for themselves, other then through a legal distribution or for a fair exchange, suggests little debate that some sort of liability should follow such conduct when corporate creditors do not get paid. Why has there been acceptance in the United States and in many other nations of the conclusion that this liability should be to pay the corporation's debts, rather than just put back any amounts inappropriately taken? Interestingly, in Germany, whether the court will impose liability for the corporation's debts, rather than simply require repayment of amounts improperly taken, depends upon whether it is possible to trace (and hence just repay) specific improper withdrawals, or whether the absence of accurate books and records, coupled with commingling of corporate and personal funds, renders such a targeted remedy impossible. *E.g.*, Alting, *supra* at 215–216.

(v) *Subordination of Stockholder Loans*

As illustrated by the facts in *Abu–Nassar*, owners of a closely held corporation often loan money to the company. As suggested by the court's opinion in *Abu–Nassar*, a court might view the need for such loans as evidence of inadequate capitalization, and thus pierce the corporate veil. In countries with a recapitalize or liquidate rule, such loans might, as apparently they did in *Abu–Nassar*, enable directors to avoid having the company file bankruptcy as soon as the company becomes insolvent. In this event, French courts not only have imposed liability on directors for not promptly complying with their duty to file bankruptcy, but also have denied claims for repayment of the loans. *E.g.*, Lutter, *supra* at 37. While not addressed by the court in *Abu–Nassar*, one additional protection for creditors sometimes applied by courts in the United States is to deny repayment of stockholder loans by a bankrupt corporation until after the company pays off its outside creditors. Invoking this remedy of "equitable subordination" depends upon the same sort of factors—such as inadequate capitalization or suspicious self-dealing—that can lead to piercing. A number of other nations, such as Germany, also use this remedy on a selective basis. *Id.* at 37–38. Greece adopted a more radical approach to stockholder loans. The Greek statute governing private companies automatically subordinates all loans from stockholders so that the company can only repay such loans after debts owed to non-stockholders. Limited Liability Company Act (Greece), art. 32. Is there some reason for insisting that stockholders always stand last in line to recover from a bankrupt company, even if they "loan" money to their corporation?

(vi) *Type of Business Restrictions*

The Lebanese statute in *Abu–Nassar* restricted brokerage businesses from operating as a limited liability company. Are there some businesses for which the owners should not have limited liability for debts of the business?

3.   Do the specific disparities when it comes to these approaches to creditor protection between corporate laws in the United States versus corporate laws in many other nations reflect broader policy and even cultural differences? Consider the following possibilities:

(i) *Civil versus common law traditions*: Do some of the disparities seem to reflect a philosophy of providing more precise standards in statutes and less discretion for judges in civil law jurisdictions versus allowing courts greater latitude to apply flexible standards in common law countries?

(ii) *Need for rules versus confidence in markets*: Do some of the disparities seem to reflect different views of whether creditors can look out for themselves when dealing with corporations?

(iii) *Creditor friendly versus debtor friendly*: Do some of the disparities seem to reflect greater concerns for creditor interests in some jurisdictions and greater concerns for corporate debtor interests in other jurisdictions? If so, could these disparities, in turn, both reflect and promote greater funding of corporations through debt financing in nations with creditor friendly laws, and greater funding of corporations through stock offerings in nations with debtor friendly laws?

CRAIG v. LAKE ASBESTOS OF QUEBEC, LTD.
843 F.2d 145 (3d Cir. 1988).

I. *Issue*

The district court held, following a trial on the issue, that appellant Charter Consolidated P.L.C. was liable under New Jersey law for the tort obligations of its subsidiary Cape Industries, P.L.C. on an "*alter ego* "or "piercing the corporate veil" theory. Because we conclude that New Jersey law does not allow for piercing the corporate veil absent a greater degree of domination of the subsidiary by its parent than that found here by the district court, we will reverse.

II. *Procedural and Factual Background*

The original plaintiffs, Clarence and Duveen Craig, New Jersey citizens, brought suit in a Pennsylvania state court to recover damages for personal injuries suffered by Clarence Craig as a result of his exposure to asbestos fibers while employed at the Owens–Corning plant in Berlin, New Jersey. Ten of the eleven defendants named were companies which manufactured, sold or supplied asbestos to Owens–Corning. Included among the defendants were appellee Lake Asbestos of Quebec, Ltd. (LAQ) * * *. After the action was removed to federal court on the basis of diversity jurisdiction, defendant LAQ impleaded Charter Consolidated and five of its wholly-owned subsidiaries (hereinafter jointly "Charter") as third-party defendants, alleging that they were the "*alter ego* entities" of certain of the suppliers of asbestos to Owens–Corning, specifically Cape Industries and several subsidiaries of Cape (hereinafter jointly "Cape"), and therefore jointly and/or severally liable with LAQ for plaintiff's injuries or liable over to LAQ for contribution or indemnity. Cape itself was not made a defendant either by the Craigs or by LAQ.

All the original defendants settled with plaintiffs, including LAQ which settled conditionally so as to maintain its third-party action against Charter. LAQ and Charter stipulated that the third-party action would be tried by the court without a jury, and that the sole issue tried would be whether Charter was responsible for the liability share of Cape as though Cape had been found to be liable to Craig. * * *

The following relevant facts are not disputed: Charter is a publicly held investment holding and finance company; Cape also is a publicly owned holding company. Both are incorporated under the laws of the United Kingdom and have their principal places of business in England. Through its subsidiaries, Cape engaged until 1979 in the mining of asbestos in South Africa and the distribution of that product to the industrial market. Between 1953 and 1978, Cape's wholly-owned subsidiary [North American Asbestos Corporation (NAAC)] sold asbestos fiber in the United States[, including to Owens–Corning]. [Under their stipulation, the parties agreed to proceed as if Cape had been found to be the alter ego of NAAC.]

Charter, through a subsidiary, acquired a 16% interest in Cape in 1965, which it expanded by gradual purchases and a 1969 tender offer until, by 1978, it held 67.3% of Cape's outstanding shares. From 1965 to 1969 Charter placed two of its own executives on Cape's Board of Directors. In 1969, after Charter acquired a majority of Cape's shares, Charter nominated a third director onto that Board, and has since that time, except for a brief period, maintained three directors on Cape's Board. During these years, Cape's Board consisted of between ten and fourteen directors. The majority were Cape employees, but there were two and sometimes three outside directors connected with neither Cape nor Charter. The managing director of Cape, originally R.H. Dent and later G.A. Higham, sat on the Board of Charter.

In 1973, Cape and its wholly-owned subsidiary NAAC were named as defendants in two asbestos injury suits filed in Texas. Cape unsuccessfully challenged jurisdiction. Ultimately, these cases were settled for $20 million, with Cape and NAAC responsible for $5.2 million. Thereafter, Cape declined to defend other asbestos litigation in the United States, permitting default judgments totaling $78 million to be entered against it.

NAAC was dissolved in 1978; in its place was formed the Continental Products Corporation (CPC), which ostensibly had no ties to Cape. However, Charles G. Morgan, NAAC's former president, was the president and sole shareholder of CPC, which had received its start-up funds through Cape's payment of "termination compensation" to Morgan. CPC, which received its shipments of asbestos from Cape through a newly formed corporation in Liechtenstein, distributed asbestos to the former customers of NAAC in the United States for several years until terminating business in 1981. * * * As a result of these actions, Cape has apparently been able to avoid paying anything toward the injury claims of asbestos victims.

* * *

V. *Discussion*

A federal court sitting in diversity must apply the state substantive law as pronounced by the state's highest court * * *. Fortunately for us in this case, * * * the New Jersey Supreme Court has recently clearly and definitively set forth New Jersey law on piercing the corporate veil. *See State, Dep't of Environ. Protection v. Ventron Corp.,* 94 N.J. at 499–501, 468 A.2d at 164–65 (1983).[2]

Ventron presented a situation comparable to that here because New Jersey's Department of Environmental Protection sought to impose liability on a parent corporation for the dumping of toxic wastes by its wholly-owned subsidiary. The New Jersey trial court, affirmed on this issue by the Appellate Division, had pierced the parent's corporate veil and held the parent liable for the pollution caused by the subsidiary. The New Jersey Supreme Court expressly disagreed with the reasoning of those courts. The court stated: "We begin with the fundamental propositions that a corporation is a separate entity from its shareholders, * * * and that a primary reason for incorporation is the insulation of shareholders from the liabilities of the corporate enterprise." * * * It continued, "[e]ven in the case of a parent corporation and its wholly-owned subsidiary, limited liability normally will not be abrogated." * * * It explained that the corporate veil may be pierced only where (1) "the parent so dominated the subsidiary that it had no separate existence but was merely a conduit for the parent" and (2) "the parent has abused the

---

2. In light of our disposition of the case we need not reach the issue of whether the district court correctly chose to apply New Jersey law as opposed to United Kingdom law. LAQ argued that New Jersey law should apply, and we accept that view in considering the case.

privilege of incorporation by using the subsidiary to perpetrate a fraud or injustice, or otherwise to circumvent the law." * * * New Jersey is thus in line with the approach taken generally on this issue.

We accept for purposes of this appeal the district court's findings and conclusion that Cape's scheme to avoid asbestos-injury liability in the United States constituted the type of "fraud or injustice" that would satisfy that element of the standard for piercing the corporate veil. Although we therefore do not reach the legal issue of the type of fraud required, we appreciate the district court's sensitivity to the asbestos victim's lack of redress under a scenario whereby the seller of the injurious material (NAAC) is dissolved, its parent (Cape) suffers default judgments that may be uncollectible, and nevertheless the product from the same source continues to be sold and distributed in the United States. We comment merely that evasion of tort liability has never, in itself, been sufficient basis to disregard corporate separateness.

We turn instead to consider whether the evidence produced of record shows the type of control necessary to constitute Cape the *alter ego* of Charter. * * * *Ventron* makes clear that piercing the corporate veil "depends on" a finding of dominance. Only after there has been such a finding does one reach the fraud or injustice issue.

The control which a parent must exercise over a subsidiary so as to warrant piercing the veil between them is more than "mere majority or complete stock control;" instead it is "complete domination, not only of finances but of policy and business practice in respect to the transaction attacked so that the corporate entity as to this transaction had at the time no separate mind, will or existence of its own." * * *

It is assumed to be the norm that a parent will have "not only . . . the potential to exercise control [over the subsidiary], but to exercise it to a substantial degree." It is patently clear since *Ventron* that in New Jersey even the exercise of significant control by the parent over the subsidiary will not suffice to pierce the corporate veil. The relationship between the parent and subsidiary in *Ventron* was that Velsicol owned 100% of the Wood Ridge stock, all directors of Wood Ridge were officers of Velsicol, and the Wood Ridge board of directors met monthly in the Velsicol offices in Chicago. * * *

Based on these facts, the New Jersey Supreme Court found that the record supported the lower court's conclusion that the "Velsicol [the parent corporation] personnel, directors and officers were constantly involved in the day-to-day operations of the business of [Wood Ridge] [the subsidiary]." Nonetheless, the Supreme Court held "those conclusions are not sufficient to support the further conclusion that the intrusion of Velsicol into Wood Ridge's affairs reached the point of dominance." Because of both the lack of the requisite "dominance" and because the *Ventron* court thought that the subsidiary had not been incorporated for an "unlawful purpose," the Court decided that the common-law doctrine of piercing the corporate veil was not applicable.[3]

It is against the standard established in the *Ventron* decision that we must examine the conclusion of the district court that sufficient control was exercised by Charter over Cape to pierce the corporate veil under New Jersey law. The district court based its conclusion on findings of fact regarding Charter's publicly announced intentions in connection with its tender offer to "control" Cape and use it to expand Charter's industrial activities; on Charter's involvement in Cape's financial and management affairs; on the presence of three Charter nominees on Cape's Board; and on Charter's ownership of a majority of Cape's stock and its ability to exercise control through that ownership if it so wished.[5]

It is to be expected that a corporation seeking to acquire majority ownership of another will seek to achieve control. Thus, Charter's statements upon which the district court relied, including particularly the statement that Charter "takes direct management responsibility for mining operations, both in the U.K. and overseas," when viewed in the context of a takeover bid, do not add to the inquiry of how it exercised the control it eventually achieved. Indeed, R.H. Dent, the Chairman of Cape who had opposed the takeover, remained in that position for 10 years following the acquisition.

The district court also relied on its finding of "much evidence of Charter's widespread involvement in Cape's financial and management decisions." The court looked to the evidence that Charter had promised to give Cape "strong financial backing," Cape "routinely consulted Charter on 'financial decisions of a major character,'" "Charter arranged financing for various Cape projects, and Cape agreed to discuss its dividend recommendations with Charter before they were presented to Cape's Board. In addition, a Charter statement revealed its plan to "maintain ... close scrutiny of new capital expenditure projects" * * *; Charter on at least one occasion expressed displeasure to the Cape Board when the Cape Board decided to make an acquisition without consulting Charter; Cape subsequently agreed that it would consider "Charter's policy towards the size of its shareholding in Cape" when making future acquisition decisions; the Chairman of Cape, R.H. Dent, who also sat on Charter's Board, regularly reported to Charter on Cape's financial re-

---

3. In discussing the significance of the *Ventron* case, the district court here believed that it was the absence of fraud or injustice, not the absence of sufficient control by the parent over the subsidiary, that was determinative of the New Jersey Court's decision not to pierce the corporate veil. In light of the explicit statement by the *Ventron* court that the parent's intrusion into the affairs of the subsidiary did not reach the point of dominance, we cannot agree. Both the elements of "control" and injustice were seen as essential to justify piercing the corporate veil in *Ventron,* and both were found to be lacking by the Court.

5. Although the district court stated that while "[t]he fraudulent or inequitable acts upon which LAQ bases its requests for relief are primarily those of Cape," it also found, rejecting the credibility of the Charter witnesses, that the board members, including Charter's nominee directors, knew of Cape's scheme to avoid liability prior to the board meeting at which the decision to dissolve NAAC was formally adopted. Because we are accepting the district court's findings and conclusions of fraudulent conduct for purposes of this appeal, it is not necessary for us to decide if this is sufficient to tarnish Charter with Cape's fraud.

sults; and Dent sought to discuss with Charter his remaining as Chairman of Cape beyond the age of 60.

The involvement in Cape's financial and managerial affairs fails to rise to the high standard of domination necessary to pierce the corporate veil set out in *Ventron*. There, although the parent was *"constantly involved in the day-to-day business"* of its subsidiary, the Court held that the control over the subsidiary had not reached the required "point of dominance." In this case, there is no evidence that Charter's intrusion into Cape's affairs is even "constant" or day-to-day. Moreover, and significantly, the district court found that "[t]he two corporate groups each maintained separate books, records, bank accounts, offices and staff; each consulted their own financial advisors, accountants and stockbrokers."

The district court concluded that Charter's majority share of stock ownership gave it an "omnipresence in the minds of the Cape Board members" such that Cape was nothing more than an "operating division" of Charter. However, potential control is not enough. Moreover, if the actual control exercised in *Ventron* was insufficient, the mere power to control cannot be determinative.

* * *

VI. *Conclusion*

For the reasons set forth above, the judgment of the district court will be reversed, and the case remanded to the district court for entry of judgment in favor of Charter.

Note

Would there have been any different result if the court in *Craig* applied English instead of New Jersey law? The answer to this question—as well as the explanation of how Cape Industries was able to avoid paying the default judgments entered against it in the United States—can be found in the following opinion from the British court that dealt with an effort to enforce these judgments.

ADAMS v. CAPE INDUSTRIES

2 W.L.R. 657, 1989 WL 651250 (C.A.1990).

* * *

The question in the present case is whether Cape and Capasco were, when the Tyler 2 actions [class actions brought in Illinois against Cape Industries and its subsidiaries based upon injuries resulting from asbestos exposure] were instituted, resident or present in Illinois. Reliance is placed by the plaintiffs on the activities and presence first of N.A.A.C. and later of C.P.C. at their respective Illinois offices at 150, North Wacker Drive, Chicago. I must describe the relevant facts and then endeavour to apply to those facts the principles established by the authorities to which I have referred. The object of doing so is to decide whether the United States federal court was entitled, on a territorial basis, to assume jurisdiction over Cape and Capasco in the Tyler 2 actions.

* * * Cape, the parent company, was incorporated in 1893. The amosite mines at Penge, in the Transvaal, were owned and worked by Egnep, a wholly owned subsidiary of Casap. The first Tyler 2 action, the Ray action, was commenced in April 1978. Since 1975 Casap had been a wholly owned subsidiary of C.I.O.L. which, in turn, was a wholly owned subsidiary of Cape. [Before 1975, Casap was simply a wholly owned subsidiary of Cape.] N.A.A.C. incorporated in 1953 as a wholly owned subsidiary of Cape, and from November 1975 a wholly owned subsidiary of C.I.O.L., was the marketing agent of the Cape group in the United States. Capasco, incorporated in 1958 or 1959, was a wholly owned subsidiary of Cape and was responsible for the supply, marketing and sales promotion throughout the world of Cape asbestos and asbestos products.

* * * N.A.A.C. had offices on the fifth floor of 150, North Wacker Drive, Chicago. N.A.A.C. was the lessee and the rent was paid by N.A.A.C. The office furniture and fittings were owned by N.A.A.C. N.A.A.C. maintained a staff of some four people. Mr. Morgan[, a United States citizen and a resident of Illinois,] was [President of N.A.A.C. and] * * * in charge. He had, however, an * * * assistant, a Mrs. Holtze. In addition, there were two or three other office staff.

N.A.A.C.'s dominant business purpose was to assist and encourage sales in the United States of asbestos mined by the Cape subsidiaries, one of which was Egnep. Contracts with United States customers for the supply of asbestos were entered into by Egnep or Casap—I am not clear which and it does not matter. The contracts tended to be long term but did not usually specify the quantity of asbestos to be sold. The practice was for the United States customer to specify from time to time the quantity of asbestos it wished to purchase and the time when it desired delivery to be made. This information would be conveyed via N.A.A.C. to Casap and Egnep. * * * Shipping arrangements and delivery dates would be arranged by Casap or Egnep and communicated to the United States customer via N.A.A.C. The vagaries of production in the mines had the consequence that Egnep was not always able to provide the United States customer with the full amount of asbestos that had been ordered. When a shortfall between the customers' requirements and Egnep's delivery capacity emerged, N.A.A.C. would endeavour to fill the gap by purchasing asbestos from United States Government stocks and selling the asbestos to the United States customers.

These were the two main forms of business carried on by N.A.A.C. First, it acted as intermediary in respect of contracts between the United States customers and Egnep. For these services it received a commission from Casap. Secondly, N.A.A.C. sold asbestos to United States customers in order from time to time to supplement sales from Egnep. In respect of these transactions N.A.A.C. contracted, both in purchasing the asbestos and in selling on to the United States customers, as principal. * * * N.A.A.C. also, it seems from the evidence, from time to time purchased asbestos from Egnep or Casap and sold on to United States customers. These purchases and sales it transacted as principal. For the purpose of storing asbestos which it had purchased, whether from United States Government stocks or from Egnep or Casap, N.A.A.C. rented warehousing facilities in the United States. These facilities were in N.A.A.C.'s name and were paid for by N.A.A.C.

Prior to 11 July 1975 the board of directors of N.A.A.C. included two senior officers of Cape. Until 1974 a Mr. Dent, chief executive of Cape, was chairman of N.A.A.C. In 1979, however, Mr. Higham succeeded Mr. Dent as chief executive of Cape and succeeded also to the chairmanship of N.A.A.C. The other Cape director of N.A.A.C. was Dr. Gaze who was, at all material times, chairman of Capasco and an executive director of Cape. In July 1975 Mr. Higham and Dr. Gaze resigned from the board of N.A.A.C. This change was directly attributable to the involvement of Cape and Capasco in the Tyler 1 actions [earlier asbestos-related injury class actions settled by Cape] and was explained thus by Mr. Morgan in a deposition he gave in the Tyler 1 actions. The intention, he said, was

> "to dissociate the parent company as fully as possible from the operating companies ... It does not imply any change whatever in the method of operation or the present responsibilities of individuals concerned ... "

The "method of operation" and "the present responsibilities" of, in particular, Mr. Morgan, did not permit either N.A.A.C. or Mr. Morgan, its chief executive, to bind Cape, Capasco, Casap or Egnep, or any other of the Cape subsidiaries to any contract for the supply or sale of asbestos. * * * There is no doubt, on the other hand, that N.A.A.C. did constitute the channel of communication between United States customers * * * and Capasco or Casap. There is undoubtedly a sense in which N.A.A.C. was, if the Cape group of companies is viewed as a whole, part of the selling organization of the group and Cape's agent in the United States.

There is also evidence, as perhaps might be expected, that the corporate, as opposed to commercial, activities of N.A.A.C. were controlled by Cape. Thus, each year an indication would come from Cape as to the dividend that N.A.A.C. was to declare. The correspondence reveals some argument and representations from Mr. Morgan regarding the amount of the suggested dividend but, in the last resort, and subject to compliance with Illinois law, the parent company was in a position to and did direct the level of the dividend. In addition, the financial controllers in London were consulted about the level of borrowing permitted to N.A.A.C. in each financial year. This corporate financial control exercised by a parent company over its subsidiary is, in my view, no more and no less than one would expect to find in a group of companies such as the Cape group. There is, however, no evidence of any like control exercised by

Cape and Capasco over the conduct by N.A.A.C. of its commercial activities. Mr. Morgan was in executive control of N.A.A.C.'s conduct of its business. Both Dr. Gaze and, to a lesser extent, Mr. Higham, visited the United States from time to time, discussed with United States customers their asbestos supply requirements and dealt with their complaints in that regard. They did so, not as directors of N.A.A.C. but as directors and representatives of Cape or Capasco.

* * *

[The plaintiffs' attorney] argued that, on the facts of this case, N.A.A.C. should be treated as Cape's alter ego in Illinois or, alternatively, that the corporate veil distinguishing N.A.A.C. from Cape should be lifted. There is no reasonable basis, in my view, for regarding N.A.A.C. as the alter ego of Cape. N.A.A.C. was an Illinois corporation, carrying on business in the United States from which it earned profits and on which it paid United States taxes. Its debtors were *its* debtors, not Cape's debtors. Its creditors were *its* creditors, not Cape's creditors. Cape was not taxed in the United Kingdom or in the United States on N.A.A.C.'s profits. The return to N.A.A.C.'s shareholders took the form of an annual dividend passed by a resolution of N.A.A.C.'s board of directors. The corporate forms applicable to N.A.A.C. as a separate legal entity were observed. N.A.A.C. made its own warehousing arrangements for the storage of its own asbestos. It had its own pension scheme for its own employees. The expression "alter ego" when used to describe the relationship between a company and its shareholders is not a term of art and can bear a flexible meaning. But I do not think it is in the least apt to describe the relationship between N.A.A.C. and Cape.

The question whether the corporate veil should be lifted is more difficult. It is, I think, one which raises an issue of general importance. Is a parent company to be treated, for jurisdiction purposes, as resident in a country in which its wholly owned subsidiary is resident and carries on business? Should the answer be dependent on whether the subsidiary's business is associated with and, in a group sense, a part of the business of the parent company?

[The plaintiffs' attorney] argued the point by concentrating on the economic unity of the asbestos trade carried on by the Cape group. N.A.A.C. was a non-autonomous part of the Cape group which, as a unit, was mining and marketing asbestos. So, he argued, N.A.A.C.'s presence and business activity at 150, North Wacker Drive should be regarded as the presence and business activity of Cape.

* * *

The approach to be adopted to parent companies trading through subsidiaries was considered by Roskill L.J. in The Albazero [1977] A.C. 774. He said, at p. 807:

> "each company in a group of companies (a relatively modern concept) is a separate legal entity possessed of separate legal rights and liabilities * * *."

* * *

In Bank of Tokyo Ltd. v. Karoon [1987] A.C. 45, 53 Ackner L.J. said:

* * *

"[The plaintiff's attorney] suggested beguilingly that it would be technical for us to distinguish between parent and subsidiary company in this context; economically, he said, they were one. But we are concerned not with economics but with law. The distinction between the two is, in law, fundamental and cannot here be bridged."

These statements of principle seem to me to be an answer to the submission that in the present case the separate corporate identity of N.A.A.C. should be ignored and that the corporate veil should be lifted. On the facts of this case neither Cape nor Capasco had an office in Illinois. The 150, North Wacker Drive offices were N.A.A.C.'s offices. N.A.A.C.'s business was its own business, not the business of Cape or of Capasco. N.A.A.C. had no authority to contract on behalf of Cape or Capasco or any other company in the Cape group. Accordingly, in my judgment, the presence of N.A.A.C. at 150, North Wacker Drive, Chicago, Illinois, did not constitute the presence in Illinois of Cape or of Capasco so as to subject them, on a territorial basis, to the jurisdiction of United States courts.

* * *

Notes

1. *Adams* deals with piercing the corporate veil for the purpose of asserting jurisdiction over the parent corporation based upon the subsidiary's presence in the state or nation of the court in which the suit is brought, rather than piercing for the purpose of imposing liability upon the parent for the debts of the subsidiary (as in *Craig*). Should the analysis of these issues be entirely distinct? After all, what is the practical problem posed by a rule under which a court would pierce to impose liability upon a foreign parent corporation, but would not pierce in order to assert jurisdiction over the parent? What is the practical result of a rule under which a court would pierce in order to assert jurisdiction, but would not pierce in order to hold the parent liable for the debts of the subsidiary?

2. *Adams* refused to pierce N.A.A.C. despite a set of facts under which Charter's attorneys were willing to concede that N.A.A.C. would be considered Cape's alter ego under New Jersey law. Does the English court's decision in *Adams* support the notion that English courts are more reluctant to pierce the corporate veil than are their American cousins? What is the implication of the English court's decision in *Adams* as far as the ability of multinational corporations to place dangerous products into the stream of international commerce, while avoiding risking assets beyond that of a subsidiary with leased office space, all of four employees, and an uncertain amount of liability insurance?

3. Turning from English common law to continental civil law approaches, German law has attracted considerable attention because of its

unique statutory approach to liability in corporate groups (referred to in German as Konzern).

CARSTON ALTING, PIERCING THE CORPORATE VEIL IN AMERICAN AND GERMAN LAW— LIABILITY OF INDIVIDUALS AND ENTITIES: A COMPARATIVE VIEW

2 Tulsa J. Comp. & Int'l L. 187 (1995).

* * *

C. German Law (Konzernrecht)

1. General

The German law of affiliated entities is based on statutory provisions embodied in AktG [the German marketable stock company statute] sections 15–19 and 291–32. * * *

Although AktG sections 15–19 contain four different types of parent-subsidiary relations all require an Aktiengesellschaft [a marketable stock company, as opposed to a private company (a GmbH)] being dominated by another "Unternehmer," an entity or person pursuing business interests referred to as "entrepreneur."

* * *

2. Contractual Konzern-Vertragskonzern

* * *

Under AktG section 291, paragraph 1, an Aktiengesellschaft may submit itself through an explicit domination agreement to another company's direction. * * * [T]he two entities are referred to as a Vertragskonzern or contractual Konzern.

AktG section 308 enables the parent corporation [in a contractual Konzern] to instruct the board of directors of the Aktiengesellschaft. This power includes giving instructions that are detrimental to the subsidiary.

* * *

From a creditor's point of view, sections 302 and 303 of the AktG are * * * significant * * *. AktG section 302 states that the parent corporation [in a contractual Konzern] is obliged to pay for all losses the dominated Aktiengesellschaft incurred in a taxable year. Thus, it can be said that a subsidiary's creditor is a creditor of the Konzern [the affiliated group], its only concern has to be whether the Konzern is able to meet the subsidiary's obligations. After termination of a contractual Konzern, a creditor is protected by AktG section 303, which states the parent's obligation to provide guarantees amounting to the creditors' claims against the subsidiary.

* * *

3. DE FACTO KONZERN

The advantage of a domination agreement under German law is that there is statutory certainty as to the parties' duties and liabilities, especially with respect to the dominating company's assumption of obligations (AktG sections 302 and 303) which exist regardless of any specified damage caused to creditors by the control. However, entities are also affiliated without explicit agreements. In these situations, a court must investigate whether an exercised control was sufficiently tight and disadvantageous to the subsidiary to justify parent's liability. In the absence of domination agreements, German corporate law distinguishes between de facto Konzern and qualified * * * de facto Konzern, the latter having been defined by the courts.

* * *

If the dominated company is an Aktiengesellschaft, AktG sections 311 and 317 are applicable. These sections provide that the parent is liable to the subsidiary for all losses and damages incurred by the subsidiary in transactions where the parent is responsible. A subsidiary, a shareholder, or the subsidiary's creditors may bring a claim. In order to ascertain whether damages have occurred, AktG section 312 states that the subsidiary's board in a dependency report must list and describe all transactions entered into with the parent, affiliated companies, or with other legal subjects on behalf of the parent.

* * *

Although a dependent company or its shareholders may have a claim against the parent, the imposition of liability in de facto domination is very difficult to realize. The difficulty lies in singling out specific transactions detrimental to the subsidiary, despite the dependency report found in AktG section 312. A shareholder or creditor, as plaintiff, must have knowledge of the facts that caused damage to the subsidiary.

* * *

4. QUALIFIED DE FACTO KONZERN

German courts and commentators agree[d] that qualified de facto domination requires special protection for creditors. Qualified domination refers to situations where the parent company permanently interferes with a subsidiary's conduct in an unrestricted manner. It is no longer possible to single out particular transactions detrimental to the subsidiary as in a de facto Konzern. The situation is similar to a contractual Konzern, and the relevant statutory rules of the Aktiengesetz can be applied by analogy. Contrasted to a de facto Konzern, the main difference is the presumption that the parent's control is detrimental because of its total domination. The parent's liability, accordingly, exists because of the given circumstances, regardless of its intent or the specified damages incurred by the subsidiary.

* * *

However, most recently the Bundesgerichtshof [the German high court] changed its position, holding that circumstances indicating comprehensive control are not sufficient to justify the imposition of shareholder liability. The court now requires an abusive exertion of control.

The following cases decided by the Bundesgerichtshof provide illustrations. They also show that the court has taken different approaches over the years.

In [a] famous case, referred to as Autokran,[510] the plaintiff entered into leasing contracts with seven GmbHs, all of which were dominated and managed by the defendant * * *. All the financial management, including books and minutes, was handled by a separate GmbH that was also controlled by the defendant. Furthermore, the latter holding company held contracts with all the other GmbHs, according to which the holding GmbH was entitled to all of the other entities' claims against their clients including all the profit. As compensation, the holding GmbH assumed all debts and obligations, such as wages, of the other companies. When the companies defaulted on the lease payments, the plaintiff terminated the contracts and obtained judgments against the debtor companies amounting to DM 700,000. However, the plaintiff collected only DM 44,000 from the debtors and brought suit against the defendant.

The Bundesgerichtshof, confirming that an individual can be regarded as an entrepreneur under AktG section 18, argued for a qualified de facto Konzern because of the defendant's tight domination of his companies. The court applied AktG section 303 by analogy and held the defendant liable. Moreover, the plaintiff had a direct claim against the defendant because the debtor entities had been unable to make payments.

* * *

In Tiefbau,[520] the Bundesgerichtshof again decided a case involving a qualified de facto Konzern. The defendant-bank caused a sole proprietor debtor, owning and managing a construction business to convert into a GmbH when the business defaulted on bank loans. The bank subsequently controlled and dominated the GmbH. The court held the defendant-bank liable as one of several owners of the newly created GmbH because it controlled all financial matters. The defendant under AktG section 302, applied by analogy, assumed all losses and debts of the GmbH. * * * However, the court allowed a parent company to prove that the subsidiary's losses were not caused by its control and management.

510. Autokran, [Case Commentary] 1986 NJW 188.

520. Tiefbau, [Case Commentary] 1989 NJW 1800.

In Video,[528] the Bundesgerichtshof held for a qualified de facto Konzern and imposed liability on the defendant parent. The plaintiff was in the business of copying videos and had a claim for DM 1.4 million against a GmbH owned and managed by the defendant. * * * The court again ruled that the defendant, as an individual entrepreneur, met the requirements of a Konzern as defined in AktG section 18. Furthermore, the court found a qualified de facto Konzern to be present since the defendant was manager and sole owner of the debtor GmbH. The court held the defendant liable under AktG section 303. * * *

Finally, the court decided TBB[533] where the defendant was sole manager of the debtor construction company, a GmbH owned by his wife. The court first held that it was possible to impute the wife's position to the defendant if he had completely controlled the debtor entity and to view him as the factual member of GmbH. The court then, in contrast to the decisions in Video and Autokran, took a different approach and clarified its previous holdings. Following the court, the defendant, despite extensive domination, could only be personally liable if control of the GmbH was abusive. Abuse, according to the court, would require an exertion of control that disregarded the dominated entity's interests in such a way that it was impossible to compensate single disadvantages suffered by the GmbH. Furthermore, with respect to rules of burden of proof and presentation of facts, the court required the plaintiff only to establish a prima facia case. Consequently, the defendant, having all the inside knowledge, had to show sufficient facts under which he would not be liable. Since the facts were insufficiently investigated and the court had adopted new rules, the case was remanded for further proceedings.

* * *

Note

The German law governing corporate groups (Konzern) has attracted considerable attention because of its heavily statutory and categorical (or very "German" as the wag would say) set of rules especially designed for corporate groups. Yet, how significant is the categorization established by the German statute?

Start with the "contractual Konzern". How many parent corporations would one expect to enter contracts with their subsidiaries allowing the parents to control the subsidiaries without regard to the subsidiaries' interests, if the quid pro quo is that the parents must make up any business losses the subsidiaries suffer each year? After all, the practical effect of this is to eliminate limited liability.

As discussed in Chapter V, the key provision in the German statute governing "defacto Konzern"—which requires the parent to compensate the subsidiary for any disadvantageous transaction between the parent and the subsidiary—may not be that much different from obligations imposed as part

---

528. Video, [Case Commentary] 1991 NJW 3142.   **533.** TBB, [Case Commentary] 1993 NJW 1200.

of fiduciary duties in the United States. The problem, as stated in the article excerpted above, is to prove that a transaction between parent and subsidiary was disadvantageous (and caused damage) to the subsidiary. The "domination report", which the German statute obligates the subsidiary's board to prepare, was supposed to address this problem by disclosing and analyzing all transactions between parent and subsidiary; but has not worked out as well as expected. *E.g.*, Peter Hommelhoff, *Protection of Minority Shareholders, Investors and Creditors in Corporate Groups: the Strengths and Weaknesses of German Corporate Group Law*, 2 Eur. Bus. Org. L. Rev. 61, 68–69 (2001).

Hence, the most significant part of the German law of corporate groups may have been the liability imposed upon the parent corporation (or, in a number of cases, controlling individual) of a "qualified defacto Konzern". Notice that this is a judicial creation; albeit the German courts ostensibly reasoned by analogy to the statutory category of contractual Konzern. Notice also the issue—whether the control must be abusive—upon which the German cases seem to have changed the rule when it comes to determining whether liability as a qualified defacto Konzern exists.

In fact, perhaps the real utility of looking at the German law of corporate groups may come not from asking when, but rather why, it seeks to impose liability upon a parent corporation for the debts of a subsidiary. Is the rationale behind the German law simply that a corporation (or an individual) who controls another corporation ought to pay the controlled company's debts; or is the rationale based upon a concern that a corporation (or an individual), who controls another corporation, might be tempted to abuse the control by sacrificing the interest of the controlled corporation (and, in turn, the ability of the controlled corporation to pay its debts) through actions that favor the controlling party? If the real concern is with abuse of control, what role does the difficulty creditors and minority shareholders might have in establishing such abuse play in the specific rules established by German law?

In 2001, the German law moved decisively away (at least for the time being) from any notion that control alone could produce liability:

RENE REICH–GRAEFE, CHANGING PARADIGMS: THE LIABILITY OF CORPORATE GROUPS IN GERMANY

37 Conn. L. Rev. 785 (2005).

* * *

[T]he qualified de facto group doctrine * * * received a major setback in September 2001 when the Federal Supreme Court handed down a new landmark decision regarding the liability of corporate groups, the so-called *Bremer Vulkan* decision.[59] Bremer Vulkan was a major shipbuilding group in West Germany. It acquired an East German shipyard company, MTW, a GmbH, which the German Federal Govern-

---

59. BGHZ 149, 10 * * *

ment had privatized after the German reunification. As part of the acquisition, the Bremer Vulkan corporate group received substantial subsidies from the German government—officially paid to MTW, the new subsidiary—under the condition that such funds would be used exclusively for the benefit of MTW. However, since the Bremer Vulkan group had a centralized cash-management system, * * * the subsidies were paid into the collective cash pool held with the parent company's treasury instead of being kept in a separate bank account held by MTW. In 1995, the Bremer Vulkan group encountered serious financial difficulties pursuant to which the cash-pool assets were lost in their entirety, including all remaining MTW subsidies equivalent to approximately $410,000,000 at the time. MTW only survived such dispossession of its funds (as well as the subsequent bankruptcy and liquidation of the Bremer Vulkan group) because the company was re-transferred by Bremer Vulkan to the German Federal Government and was later re-privatized after the injection of additional public funds.[60]

This case seemed to have all the "bells and whistles" of parent-company liability imposed under the qualified de facto [K]on[z]ern doctrine. However, in explicitly reversing its earlier decisions, the Federal Supreme Court determined that the protective system offered by German corporate law to a controlled GmbH subsidiary against detrimental interferences by its parent shareholder should no longer follow the statutory liability system for corporate groups as created by the Stock Corporation Act for AGs and applied by analogy to GmbH subsidiaries under the qualified de facto group doctrine. Thus, with a single stroke, and without much, if any, explanation for its doctrinal reversal, the Federal Supreme Court effectively abandoned the qualified de facto group doctrine—a doctrine it had firmly established by a similar single stroke and which German corporate law had known for more than twenty years.

Instead, the Court held that such protection should be limited to the maintenance of the mandatory stated capital requirements—as applicable to the GmbH subsidiary under the German Limited Liability Company Act * * *—and a guarantee of [the subsidiary's] * * * legal and factual existence * * *. Such guarantee seemed to imply, in effect, a rather expansive duty by a parent company to show sufficient consideration * * * for the subsidiary's own, independent business interests * * *. Notwithstanding such a broad statement which, at first sight, displays a striking similarity to the legal presumption formerly employed under the qualified de facto group doctrine (i.e., lack of sufficient consideration and respect for the independent business interests and autonomy of the subsidiary), the Court in *Bremer Vulkan* merely held that a deficiency of sufficient consideration clearly existed in the case at

---

60. The plaintiff in this litigation was a special agency of the German Federal Government in charge of privatizations following the German reunification * * *; it sued several members of the management board * * * of Bremer Vulkan Verbund Aktiengesellschaft, the ultimate parent company in the Bremer Vulkan corporate group.

bar where the subsidiary was rendered incapable to pay its own debts due to the interference by the parent company.

In two subsequent decisions in 2002 (*Bremer Vulkan II* and *KBV*),[71] the Federal Supreme Court further refined and limited this completely revised liability strategy for corporate groups not governed by the Stock Corporation Act: Today, the direct liability of the parent company vis-a-vis the creditors of its subsidiary * * *[72] will only be imposed in cases in which the parent company's interference effectively destroys the continued, autonomous existence of the subsidiary ("*existenzvernichtender Eingriff*");[73] in other words, where the subsidiary will either become immediately insolvent or where the parental interference will leave the subsidiary in a financial state of inevitable and almost instant collapse. According to the Federal Supreme Court in the *KBV* decision, the doctrinal foundation and justification for such liability strategy is the parent company's abuse of the corporate form of the GmbH.

* * *

Note

Compare the current German law regarding parental liability for debts of a subsidiary, with the law in the United States. While *Craig* reflects the predominant approach in the United States, when the court holds that piercing requires both control and use of that control to commit some sort of fraud or injustice, some cases in the United States seem to suggest that control alone might be enough to pierce. What accounts for the ambivalence toward control reflected both in the split of authority in the United States and in the vacillations in German law regarding so-called qualified de facto Konzern?

Given that the law in both nations generally requires control, plus some misuse of that control, to create liability upon the parent for debts of the subsidiary, is there some difference in what constitutes an abuse of control? Would a court in the United States refuse to pierce unless a creditor of the subsidiary could establish that the parent's actions toward the subsidiary left the subsidiary immediately insolvent or facing inevitable and almost instant collapse? Do the German cases seem to be overlooking some possible concerns—such as a lack of liability insurance for tort claims, or implicit representations (such as through placing the parent corporation's name on the labels of defective products)—that might justify piercing under United States law?

---

71. BGHZ 150, 61 (*Bremer Vulkan II*); BGHZ 151, 181 (*KBV*).

72. [As opposed to] the continued internal liability of the shareholder to the GmbH only, which is complimented by the external liability of the GmbH to its creditors * * *

73. The *KBV* decision also held that the capital maintenance provisions are the *ex-* *clusive* doctrinal basis of the liability for *existenzvernichtender Eingriff*, i.e., that the Court has given up the additional "*Bestandsgarantie*" (guarantee of legal and factual existence) justification used in *Bremer Vulkan*.

Chapter IV

CORPORATE GOVERNANCE STRUCTURES

This chapter looks at the basic structures found outside the United States for governing corporations. Eschewing the details and focusing on the big picture, corporate governance around the world demonstrates a remarkable degree of convergence on the basic model, coupled with some significant divergence, both in law and in practice, on fundamental aspects of this model.

SECTION A. CONVERGENCE: THE BOARD–CENTERED MODEL OF CORPORATE GOVERNANCE

FRANKLIN A. GEVURTZ, THE EUROPEAN ORIGINS AND SPREAD OF THE CORPORATE BOARD OF DIRECTORS

33 Stetson L. Rev. 925 (2004).

* * *

Much of the study of comparative corporate governance focuses on differences between the corporate governance approaches of different nations * * *. This Article, however, focuses on a similarity: Around the world, the legal norm is that corporations are managed by, or under the direction of, a board of directors.

It is worth focusing on this similarity because it represents something of a paradox. Despite differences in culture, political institutions, and business traditions, nations have converged upon a common institution—albeit with variations—for the governance of larger business organizations. This has happened notwithstanding the historic and continuing litany of complaints to the effect that boards of directors do little.[1] * * * Given the worldwide adoption of an institution whose

---

1. * * * Nor are such complaints limited to boards in the United States. *E.g.,* Oxford Analytica Ltd, *Board Directors and Corporate Governance: Trends in G7 Coun-*

designated role seems belied by reality, it is fair to ask whose idea the corporate board of directors was and how this institution spread around the world.

* * *

Before beginning this exploration, however, it is useful to clarify essentially what a corporate board of directors is. We cannot simply rely on the label, not only because of the different languages involved in a comparative study, but also because, as one delves into the historical development of the corporate board, terminology changes. Moreover, defining the concept of a corporate board of directors presents a tricky "Goldilocks" problem. If the definition is too broad and equates any group that manages a corporation with a board, then we deprive the concept of any real meaning. After all, any company of any size will have some group of people involved in its management. Conversely, if one attempts to define the concept too precisely, then we will lose the essential universality of the institution in variations as to details, such as two-tier boards and co-determination.

The best we can do is to say that the essence of the corporate board of directors comes from three underlying concepts, which involve the relationship of the directors to the shareholders, the relationship of the directors to each other, and the relationship of the directors to the corporation's executives. The first underlying concept of corporate governance by a board of directors is that shareholders, unlike partners, do not, simply by virtue of being the owners, manage the corporation. Instead they (or, under co-determination, they and the employees) normally elect a group of persons (the directors) to have ultimate responsibility for management. The second concept is that a board of directors makes decisions by acting together as a group of peers, as opposed to the hierarchical arrangements and divisions of responsibility common among officers of any organization. The third concept is that [at least in law, if not in practice] the corporation's senior executives ultimately are answerable to the board.

tries over the Next Ten Years 267 (2d ed., Blackwell Bus.1992) *reprinted in* Robert A.G. Monks & Nell Minow, *Corporate Governance* 275 (2d ed. 2001) (explaining that, in Japan, "Formal authority is held by the company president and the board of directors, but board meetings are infrequent and decisions are rubber stamped"—in reality "Real authority is held by the company president and the operating committee," composed of the president's immediate subordinates); Monks & Minow, *supra,* at 301 (explaining that the president director-general (PDG) of French companies "wields almost unchecked control over the enterprise ... without the counter-power of the board of directors," whose composition and agenda the PDG controls; "[i]ndeed, it is regarded as 'bad manners' for the board to take a vote on a management decision"); [Mark J. Roe, *Political Preconditions to Separating Ownership from Control*, 53 Stan. L. Rev. 539, 568 (2000)] (explaining that German corporate supervisory boards meet infrequently and their information has been weak). * * *

II. THE GEOGRAPHIC ORIGIN AND THE SPREAD OF THE CORPORATE BOARD OF DIRECTORS

A. THE EARLIEST CORPORATE BOARDS

As stated at the outset of this Article, most corporations formed around the world today have boards of directors. However, if we look back to the seventeenth century, large European companies had boards of directors, but fairly large businesses owned and operated by non-Europeans did not. This suggests that the corporate board of directors originated in Europe.

1. Use of Boards by the Early European Trading Companies and Banks

The use of the term "director" to describe the members of a corporation's governing board traces [to] the 1694 charter of the Bank of England. Yet, the use of governing boards among European companies— albeit with different titles for their members—was already old by that time. To give a pair of nicely documented examples, the East India companies used governing boards as early as the beginning of the seventeenth century.

* * *

2. Non–Board Governance In Large Businesses Beyond European Influence: The Japanese Merchant House Example

At the time at which sixteenth-and seventeenth-century European trading and banking corporations already were using board governance, businesses owned and operated by non-Europeans do not seem to be employing such an institution. This is not because non-Europeans did not own and operate fairly large scale businesses. Rather, it is because larger business organizations outside the ambit of European influence utilized different management structures. The Japanese merchant houses prior to the Meiji Restoration in 1868 provide a good illustration.

* * *

The merchant house did not have a board, elected by the owners, to make decisions as a group of peers with ultimate responsibility to select and to supervise the senior management of the business. Instead, ultimate authority rested with the head of the house, to whom all employees and house members owed a duty of total obedience. * * *

B. THE SPREAD OF CORPORATE BOARDS

1. European Colonies

The spread of corporate boards to European colonies is unremarkable, especially since one of the roles of the European trading companies governed by boards was to establish colonies. * * *

The Bank of the United States, chartered in 1791 (often called the First Bank of the United States), illustrates the tendency of former colonies to copy board governance from European institutions. It seems evident that the United States' bank's twenty-five-person board was modeled on the twenty-four-person board of the Bank of England. * * *

2.   *Outside of European Colonies: The Japanese Example*

What is more interesting is the spread of corporate board governance to nations with other traditions. Once again, Japan provides a nice illustration. The development of corporate board governance in Japan came about with the introduction of the joint stock company as a form of doing business in that nation. The importation of this business form, in turn, was just one component of an effort to introduce Western technology and ideas into Japan following Meiji Restoration in 1868.

* * *

III.   WHY DID THE CORPORATE BOARD OF DIRECTORS EVIDENTLY ORIGINATE IN EUROPE AND SPREAD FROM THERE?

A.   A Traditional Story

One constant in human history is the clever invention occurring in a part of the world and then spreading throughout the globe as people in different lands copy the invention. For instance, fine porcelain arises in China and the Europeans copy the idea. * * * An obvious explanation as to why the corporate board originated in Europe and spread from there would follow along the same sort of lines: The corporate board of directors was a clever invention by the Europeans, who were looking for a mechanism to govern a business in which large numbers of individuals would make passive investments and receive shares in the venture (the joint stock company).

* * *

B.   A Revisionist Story

The problem with the story outlined above is that it is simply wrong in explaining why the corporate board of directors arose in Europe. Moreover, while the story might have some merit insofar as non-Europeans copied the corporate board based upon the assumption that it was the most efficient way to run a joint stock company, it less clear whether the story is correct as to the real impact of the corporate board. * * *

1.   *European Corporate Board Governance Prior to the Joint Stock Companies*

The reason we can conclude that Europeans did not develop the corporate board of directors to monitor management on behalf of passive investors in the joint stock company is that the board, as an institution of corporate governance, predated the invention of the joint stock company by a century or more. In fact, the English and the Dutch East India companies, with their governing boards, evolved from the so-called "regulated company"—essentially a guild whose membership consisted of merchants conducting independent operations under the company's franchise. * * *

* * * The governing board of a regulated company adopted ordinances regulating the members' activities. For example, the board of the Eastland Company adopted a regulation prohibiting members from engaging in "colouring" goods[, in other words,] selling goods of a non-member merchant as a member's own. * * * As this example illustrates, the role of a board of a regulated company was not to have overall responsibility for operating a business, but to impose rules on individual merchants in order to preserve a monopoly.

* * *

2. The Origins of Corporate Boards in Political and Cultural Ideas

Since the corporate board of directors in Europe did not start as a devise to supervise management on behalf of passive investors in a joint stock company, how did the idea originate? In fact, corporate governance by a representative board, working with a chief executive officer (a "governor" in the typical parlance of the early corporate charters), is a reflection of political practices and ideas widespread in Western Europe in the late Middle Ages. Specifically, while fictional literature may frequently picture medieval Europe as a place of autocratic governance by kings, European political ideology and practice in the late Middle Ages, although hardly democratic, often called for the use of collective governance by a body of representatives. Examples of such representative-governance ideas and practices are found in the assemblies or parliaments of medieval European kingdoms, in town councils, in governing councils for guilds, and in the Church. Given this prevalent practice, and the ideology that underlay this practice, it was natural for the early corporations to utilize board governance.

* * *

A detailed account of the underlying ideas behind these representative institutions, and how those ideas came to be manifested in the early corporate boards, is beyond the scope of this Article. For present purposes, suffice it to say that joint-stock companies arose out of regulated companies, which were little more than merchant guilds with an exclusive franchise. Hence, the linkage between board governance in the merchant guilds and in the trading companies is easy enough to understand. The merchant guilds, in turn, were closely connected with medieval European municipal governments, which, in part, explains the link between company boards, boards in merchant guilds, and town councils. Moreover, to medieval European jurists, both guilds and towns were a *universitates* (essentially, a corporation), and, as such, subject to common norms of governance with other corporations. The medieval European guilds and town councils, themselves, reflected political ideas and practices also manifested in the medieval European parliaments and in the Church councils.

* * *

Just as medieval European political ideas were the source for the corporate board, different political and cultural ideas meant the absence of a board elsewhere. The governance structure of the Japanese merchant house provides a good illustration. As discussed earlier, the merchant house was part of the organization of all four orders of Japanese society into houses, in which the head of the house was entitled to obedience. This family-oriented, hierarchical organization is consistent with Confucian values. * * *

3. The Transplant of Corporate Board Governance: Post Hoc Ergo Procter Hoc Reasoning and Culture Spread

By the nineteenth century, when the Japanese and other non-Europeans were looking at adopting the joint stock company, the history of when and why Europeans developed the corporate board was centuries old. It is doubtful how many Europeans at that point were aware of when and why the tradition of board governance started. Instead, what was visible to the Japanese and others was a form of business that had a tremendous advantage in raising capital by selling shares to large numbers of strangers, and that seemed always to have a board of directors at its helm. Hence, the Japanese and other non-Europeans did what people often do: They assumed that correlation equaled causation, and, in adopting the joint stock company, also adopted the governance structure they assumed was necessary for such companies—a board of directors.

* * *

SECTION B. DIVERGENCE

1. DIVERGENCE IN LAWS

a. Co-determination, Dutch "Structure" Companies, and other Variations in Electing Directors

As discussed above, the basic model of corporate governance posits that shareholders elect directors. Yet, one could certainly conceive of other approaches. For example, even a non-Marxist might suggest that a corporation's workers ought to elect some representatives to a corporation's board. Alternately, persons with less faith in the applicability of democratic principles to the business arena might favor a self-perpetuating board, whose members fill vacancies as needed and never must stand for re-election. Not surprisingly, laws in a few nations have provided for these different approaches.

Corporate laws in Germany and a number of other European nations provide for employee representation on corporate boards. The label for this is "co-determination"—since the notion is that both capital and labor are thereby involved in determining corporate policy. Looking at Germany for the most noted example, under the 1952 Works Council Constitution Act, all German firms with more than 500 employees (unless the firm is conducted as a sole proprietorship or a partnership composed of natural persons) must have a board, one-third of whose members are elected by the employees of the firm who work in Germany. The 1976 Co-determination Act requires all German firms with more than 2000 employees to allow the employees working in Germany to elect half of the members of the supervisory board (the size of which depends, under the Act, upon how many persons the company employs). The ability to elect half the board under the 1976 Act does not quite give parity to employees, however, since the representatives of the shareholders on the board can elect the chair, who has the power to cast a tie-breaking vote.

Would co-determination be a good system within the United States? Not surprisingly, there are mixed opinions on co-determination in Europe:

> It is very probable that labor co-determination weakens the control function of the supervisory board. This is because co-determination has led to fractionalization, which is evidenced by the firm practice of separate meetings of the shareholder and the labor sides before the board meeting and by a marked reluctance of the shareholder side to openly criticize the management board. Furthermore, it happens that much of the time spend in the supervisory board meetings is devoted to issues of particular interest to the labor side rather than to the actual supervision of business decisions and entrepreneurial planning in the company.

> Yet the voices from inside the supervisory boards are mixed. Some make clear that the input of labor in the board is important and useful. A long-time bank representative made a point of stating that, in practice, co-determination has proved to be efficient and that he had never experienced labor representatives voting against measures which were important and decisive for the future of the enterprise. * * * In my view, the evaluation may depend inter alia on two key issues: first, whether co-determination fulfills the consensus-building function between capital and labor, not only in the enterprise itself but also beyond; and second, whether the efficiency losses co-determination undoubtedly has are still outbalanced by this consensus building today when the need for quick reaction to global competition is more urgent than at any time before.

Klaus J. Hopt, *The German Two–Tier Board: Experience, Theories, Reforms*, in COMPARATIVE CORPORATE GOVERNANCE—THE STATE OF THE ART AND EMERGING RESEARCH 247–248 (1998) (Klaus J. Hopt, et al. eds.). While Professor Hopt discusses anecdotal evidence, what about more scientific studies?

The attempt to check empirically the economic effects of co-determination for supervisory boards has to struggle against a whole series of difficulties. In Germany, nearly all large companies are subject to co-determination for their supervisory boards, so that there is almost no way of comparing large companies with co-determination with those without it. On the other hand, a comparison with small companies is a problem because of the significant influence of company size on efficiency. International comparisons are not very helpful either. The objection [is] that other factors of the economic and institutional context may have been more relevant.

* * *

The studies [based upon behavioral science] discussed here suggest that co-determination has at least not had any negative effects on companies' efficiency.

Similar results were obtained in studies which [looked at firm productivity, cost and profitability].

Elmar Gerum & Helmut Wagner, *Economics of Labor Co–Determination in View of Corporate Governance* in COMPARATIVE CORPORATE GOVERNANCE—THE STATE OF THE ART AND EMERGING RESEARCH 348–351 (1998) (Klaus J. Hopt, et al. eds.)

The Netherlands is another nation that decided corporate boards should represent the interests of employees as well as shareholders. Starting in 1971, however, the Netherlands chose to implement this policy for its largest domestic companies in an usual manner. This regime, known as "structure", challenged the very notion that a board ought to be elected by anyone other than the board itself. Dutch corporations are subject to structure if they meet or exceed a certain size in terms of capital and reserves, have a works council to represent their employees, and regularly employ one hundred or more persons in the Netherlands. (Smaller Dutch companies are able to opt into the structure regime, while exemptions exist for multinational business enterprises.) Under the structure regime as it existed for over three decades, neither the shareholders nor the employees elected directors to the corporation's supervisory board. Instead, directors gained office by the process of co-option—in other words, the existing members filled any vacancies. The limit on the existing members' power of selection was that the shareholders, through their general meeting, or the employees, through their works council, could challenge the selection in an Amsterdam court. The bases for challenge included: process errors (such as the failure to announce properly the vacancy); problems with the qualifications of the selectee to make a good board member in general; and an imbalance in the overall composition of the board (for example, if all the members of the board had backgrounds in finance and none in industrial relations). *E.g.*, Martijn van Empel, *The Netherlands* in THE LEGAL BASIS OF CORPORATE GOVERNANCE IN PUBLICLY HELD CORPORATIONS: A COMPARATIVE APPROACH 140 (1998) (Arthur R. Pinto & Gustavo Visentini eds.).

What are the advantages and disadvantages of selecting board members through co-option? Removing the power of election from the shareholders presumably makes the board less responsive to pressure from the shareholders. Are there any advantages to this? Might it lead to greater "societal harmony" by increasing the prospect that those in charge of a corporation will run the company for the benefit of various stakeholders (shareholders, workers, creditors, consumers and the community in general)? Can it lead to greater economic efficiency by facilitating firm-specific efforts by employees, who otherwise might hold back for fear that a board overly responsive to shareholder pressure might sell out the employees' interests? On the other hand, what danger might exist if the board is not accountable through an electoral process to shareholders or to anyone else? Are there alternatives to the electoral process for maintaining accountability and appropriate incentives for board members?

As with co-determination, one might attempt to assess empirically the impact of structure by examining the performance of companies subject to this regime. A study commissioned by the Dutch government found poorer financial performance for companies subject to structure. William W. Bratton & James A. McCahery, *Restructuring the Relationship between Shareholders and Managers* 79 in HERPOSITIONERING VAN ONDERNEMINGEN, PREADVIEZEN VAN DE KONINKLIJKE VERENINGING VOOR DE STAATHUISHOUDKUNDE, 2001 (Utrecht: Lemma). (Recall, however, the limitations inherent in this sort of study, as noted in the quote above dealing with studies of co-determination.) Reacting in 2003 to this study, the Netherlands legislature watered down the structure regime of board selection through co-option. Now, the shareholders can vote on two-thirds of the members of the supervisory board—with the remaining one-third of the members representing the employees under a co-determination approach. Still, while the shareholders get to vote, they do not get to nominate anyone to the board. Instead, nominations remain controlled by the existing members. Civil Code Book 2, title 4, section 6, article 158. The end result is to give the shareholders a veto over, but not the right to dictate, composition of two-thirds of the supervisory board.

While the Dutch structure regime is unique, is it really all that unprecedented? Even when shareholders have the right to nominate and vote for directors, do shareholders usually select the directors—at least in large publicly held corporations? Specifically, how often do contested elections occur for positions on the board of publicly held corporations in the United States or abroad? In the absence of a choice between candidates in an election, who selects directors for corporations? How much different is this from a formal system of co-option? By the way, selection by co-option is common among boards of non-profit corporations.

One possible reason that contested elections for directors are rare in the United States is that the proxy form sent out at corporate expense only provides shareholders the option to grant or to withhold their votes for the slate of directors nominated by the current board. If other persons want to run for positions on the board, they must solicit their own proxies. By contrast, a relatively new Russian corporate statute allows shareholders with at least two percent of the stock to nominate candidates for election to the board, and requires the corporation to mail to all shareholders a ballot that contains the names of all candidates so nominated. Federal Law on Joint Stock Societies (Federal Law No. 208–3) art. 53(1), 60 (as amended). Is there any irony to the fact that the existing United States practice (unlike the Russian statute) resembles the ballot used in "elections" in the old Soviet Union, in which the voters only received the option to vote *dah* (yes) or *nyet* (no) on the slate of candidates proposed by the Communist Party?

Even if shareholders elect directors, the responsiveness of the board to the shareholders' electoral power is a function of two variables: the directors' terms in office, and whether the shareholders can remove directors before the end of the directors' terms. Generalizing quite a bit, corporate laws in different nations tend to show an inverse relationship between these two variables—the longer the directors' terms in office under the law in the nation, the more the law in the nation provides for removal before the end of the term; the shorter the term in office, the less the law provides for removal before the end of the term. *E.g.*, Henry Hansmann & Reiner Kraakman, *Basic Governance Structure* in THE ANATOMY OF CORPORATE LAW: A COMPARATIVE AND FUNCTIONAL APPROACH 37–38 (2004). Is this a coincidence, or is there an evident policy underlying this inverse relationship?

b. Two-tier Boards and other Variations in Board Structure and Function

The discussion of co-determination and structure above referred to the "supervisory board." This reflects the fact that Germany and the Netherlands, as well as some other European countries, require at least some corporations to have what is known as a two-tier board. In such an arrangement, the corporation will have a management board and a supervisory board. Rather tautologically, the management board is supposed to manage the company, while the supervisory board is supposed to supervise the management. *E.g.*, Aktiengesetz §§ 76(1), 111(1). Yet, what is the difference between managing and supervising management? In Germany, the supervisory board appoints, and can remove (but only for cause), members of the management board. *Id.* at § 84(1), (3). It represents the corporation in any dealings with members of the management board (in other words, approving conflict of interest transactions involving members of the management board). *Id.* at § 112. The supervisory board can examine books and records, appoint auditors, and call a shareholders meeting. Yet, generally, it cannot command the management board to do anything, nor even veto actions of the management board (unless the corporation's articles give the supervisory board a veto power). *Id.* at § 111(2)-(4).

This leads to the question of why have two boards (unless one simply assumes automatically that "two heads are better than one"). The answer to this question is less than straightforward, because the two-tier board weaves together a number of different ideas regarding board composition and function.

To begin with, notice the overlap between the two-tier board and co-determination. This is not a complete overlap, because many corporations (such as the German AG with less than 500 employees) must have two-tier boards even without co-determination, and some nations mandate co-determination even with single-tier (or unitary) boards. *E.g.,* Companies Act, Art. 49 (requiring co-determination on a unitary board for companies in Denmark with at least 35 employees). In fact, the two-tier board pre-dates co-determination, since long before co-determination started in 1952, the 1870 general incorporation law in Germany mandated a two-tier board for the marketable stock company (the AG). Nevertheless, the overlap between the two-tier board and co-determination is not coincidental. This is because the notion behind the two-tier board from the outset was that the supervisory boards would oversee that marketable stock companies operated in the interest of the society in general, rather than just the shareholders' interest. Hopt, *supra* at 230.

Next, notice the specific rights and functions of the supervisory board in Germany—i.e. appointing members of the management board, representing the corporation in dealing with members of the management board, examination of books and records, appointment of auditors. Is there a rough parallel between these rights and functions, and the tasks of the nominating, compensation and audit committees found on the boards of typical publicly held corporations in the United States? More broadly, do these rights and functions seem more or less to match the notion advanced by many commentators in the United States that corporate boards primarily exist to monitor management, rather than actually to manage the corporation?

Yet, to identify the functions of the supervisory board does not explain why a single board cannot perform both those functions and the basic management functions of a management board. At this point, notice that probably the most critical element of the two-tier board is to separate two different types of directors. On a unitary board, some members may be so-called inside directors—in other words, directors who are also full-time executives involved in day-to-day management of the corporation. Other directors may be so-called outside directors—in other words, directors who are not employed in managing the corporation other than serving on the board. (Outside directors may or may not be "independent" directors. For example, a lawyer whose law firm represents the corporation, or who is the personal attorney of the corporation's CEO, would be an outside director, but might not be considered all that independent from influence by the management or the CEO.) The German corporate law forbids senior executives from sitting on the supervisory board (Aktiengesetz § 105(1)), thus dividing inside and outside directors into two different boards with two different roles. Is there some reason why the tasks of the supervisory board—such as appointing those who will be responsible for actual management, approving conflict of interest transactions with managers, and appointing the auditors—should be left exclusively to outside directors meeting entirely separate and apart from the inside directors? Is there a disadvantage to creating this separation between inside and outside directors?

> In particular, it can be noted that even under the one-tier board system of the U.S. and Great Britain, the functions of management and of monitoring tend to be separated. This is done by appealing to outside directors, also called independent directors, who have specific competencies and tasks in situations of conflicts of interest and when other critical decisions have to be made. The most important advantage of the one-tier system, it is said, is that these outside directors are on the management board itself and do not form a separate organ like the supervisory board; they thus have direct access to information, management, and monitoring of the corporation. One disadvantage, as we see from the German side, is that all members of the board have been integrated into decisions that may have been incorrect. And there is no institutional distance between those board members who do the day-to-day management and those board members who monitor management.

Klause J. Hopt, *Corporate Governance in Germany* in CAPITAL MARKETS AND COMPANY LAW 303–4 (2003) (Klause J. Hopt & Eddy Wymeersch, eds.).

This discussion may suggest why, even if most corporate laws do not mandate two-tier boards, there is movement in many countries—including the United States, as most recently the result of provisions in the Sarbanes–Oxley Act—toward increasing the proportion of outside (and, indeed, independent), versus inside, directors on unitary boards, and increasing the critical role of outside directors (for example on audit and nominating committees). *E.g.*, Code de commerce, art. L 225–22 (no more than one-third of the directors of French public companies can be employed by the company); http://www.europa.eu.int/comm/internal_market/company/independence/index_en.htm (setting out a voluntary code of conduct proposed by the European Commission to ensure a strong role for non-executive directors).

Beyond the role of the board vis-a-vis managing executives, another question of board function involves the role of the board versus shareholders in making business decisions. In the United States, shareholders can veto certain major decisions of the board (such as mergers or amendments of the articles), but shareholders normally cannot command action by the board. Corporate laws in other nations are more mixed in this regard. *Compare* Eddy Wymeersch, *A Status Report on Corporate Governance Rules and Practices in Some Continental European States*, in COMPARATIVE CORPORATE GOVERNANCE—THE STATE OF THE ART AND EMERGING RESEARCH 1094 (1998) (Klaus J. Hopt, et al. eds.) (citing Netherlands and French cases for the proposition that the shareholders meeting is not entitled to give binding instructions to the board), *with* Aktiengesetz §§ 83 (management board of German public company must prepare a resolution on, and implement, matters falling within shareholder competence if commanded by vote of the shareholders meeting), 118 (listing matters within shareholder competence, including amendment of articles), 174 (shareholders meeting decides on dividends); Hansmann & Kraakman, *supra* at 47 (giving similar examples of shareholder power to command action in Japan, France and England). Is there some reason why the board should act as a "gatekeeper," who can prevent the shareholders from obtaining the corporate action the shareholders desire (at least without changing the persons who serve on the board)?

2. DIVERGENCE IN PRACTICE

BRIAN R. CHEFFINS, CORPORATE GOVERNANCE CONVERGENCE: LESSONS FROM AUSTRALIA

16 Transnat'l Law. 13 (2002).

* * *

II. The World's Rival Corporate Governance Systems

The structure of ownership and control that exists in the United States and the United Kingdom has been characterized as an "outsider/arm's-length" system. The "outsider" typology is used to describe the situation that exists because most big firms do not have "core" shareholders (e.g. family owners, affiliated firms or the state) that own enough equity to exercise "inside" influence. Instead, share ownership is typically dispersed among a large number of institutional and individual shareholders. The term "arm's-length" signifies that investors in the U.S. and the U.K. are rarely poised to intervene and take a hand in running a business. Instead, they tend to maintain their distance and give executives a free hand to manage.

Adolf Berle and Gardiner Means, in a famous book published in 1932, drew attention to the emergence of the outsider/arm's-length governance pattern in the U.S. They said there was "a separation of ownership and control" in America's larger public companies because share ownership was too widely dispersed to permit stockholders to scrutinize managerial decision-making properly. The normative implications of their analysis were widely debated in the decades that followed. Interested observers implicitly agreed, however, that the "Berle–Means corporation" must inevitably be the dominant paradigm in a market economy. According to the prevailing orthodoxy, big companies would, by virtue of economies of scale, dominate key industries. Fragmented share ownership was inevitable because a handful of wealthy individuals could not provide such firms with proper financial backing. * * *

Perhaps because of this seemingly compelling economic reasoning, Berle and Means' work fixed the image of the modern corporation as one run by professional managers who were potentially unaccountable to widely dispersed shareholders. In fact, however, the Berle–Means corporation is far from universal. While an outsider/arm's-length system of ownership and control might prevail in the U.S. and the U.K., corporate governance in continental Europe and in market-oriented economies in East Asia is organized on a much different basis. Publicly quoted companies do not play as nearly as important a role in the economy. Also, with those firms that are publicly traded, "core" shareholders are prevalent and are usually well situated to exercise considerable influence over management. The prevailing approach to corporate governance, therefore, is "insider/control-oriented."

While capitalism is organized on a different basis in continental Europe and East Asia than it is in the U.S. and the U.K., matters may well be in flux. Certainly, prior to the fall in global equity markets in 2001, there was much anecdotal evidence which suggested that some form of convergence was occurring along Anglo–American lines. For instance, frequent initial public offerings (IPOs) meant the number of listed companies was growing rapidly in continental Europe.

* * *

[I]t remains unclear whether continental Europe and market-oriented countries in Asia are in fact experiencing any sort of wholesale shift towards Anglo–American capitalism. * * *

More broadly, it cannot be taken for granted that the Berle–Means corporation will become dominant by virtue of its inherent economic advantages. Germany and Japan, both insider/control-oriented countries, seemed to be enjoying greater economic success than the U.S. during the late 1980s and early 1990s. This implied that their systems of corporate governance were fully capable of yielding results similar or even superior to the American model. Indeed, the inference some drew from Germany and Japan's economic performance was that the U.S. and the U.K. would benefit by adopting, with modifications, corporate governance features from these two countries.

Even if the Berle–Means corporation does constitute the evolutionary pinnacle, a switch to Anglo–American capitalism will not necessarily occur in countries where a different system currently prevails. Convergence may instead occur only within limits set by national contexts. For instance, Mark Roe has argued that a country's system of ownership and control is politically and ideologically contingent, instead of simply being the product of market forces. Also, various empirical studies suggest that dispersed shareholdings and strong securities markets are unlikely to become well-established in countries that do not offer significant legal protections to minority shareholders.

* * *

Notes

1. Professor Cheffins focuses on the divergence in corporate governance entailed in the vastly different abilities of shareholders to turn their voting rights into actual power over the corporation, depending upon whether all the stock is widely distributed or a relatively few shareholders hold a majority (or an otherwise controlling fraction) of the voting stock. Since this is not a difference in law, one might be tempted ask what is its relevance to law. In fact, it could be relevant in a couple of ways. To begin with, this divergence might create different dangers of abuse by those in control of the corporation, thereby necessitating different legal strategies when it comes, for example, to dealing with mismanagement by directors and controlling shareholders. In addition, Professor Cheffins points out that this divergence might, at least in part, itself be the result of divergence in law. For example, differences in laws governing the permissible investment activities of banks could have produced differences in the extent to which banks own controlling interests in corporations. More broadly, laws providing greater protection for minority shareholders could promote corporations without controlling shareholders—since such laws make controlling interests less worth having by limiting the ability of controlling shareholders to extract a disproportionate share of corporate value, and might encourage smaller investments in corporations by making such investments safer.

2. In painting the picture of a bipolar corporate world divided between "insider" and "outsider" governance systems, Professor Cheffins might be lumping together some rather different governance situations. Specifically, consider the following four situations, all of which Professor Cheffins treats as insider systems:

(i) Individual families hold controlling blocks of stock even in the largest corporations. (This is common in numerous countries, including Sweden, Italy and South East Asian countries.)

(ii) Banks, either by virtue of their own stock holdings, or by virtue of having proxies to vote share certificates left on deposit with the bank, have significant influence on the boards of major corporations. (This is common, albeit decreasingly so, in Germany.)

(iii) A group of companies having various commercial relationships with each other (e.g., bank/borrower, vendor/buyer) hold controlling blocks of stock in each other. (This is common in Japan.)

(iv) The government holds a controlling interest in many of the largest corporations. (This is common in France and China.)

Would you expect the presence of these four different types of controlling shareholders to lead these corporations to act in different ways? Specifically, do families, banks, and governments share the same motivations when it comes to the actions of corporations in which they exercise control? If a group of corporations own stock in one another, who decides how the stock is voted? Who does this leave in charge?

Chapter V

MISMANAGEMENT BY DIRECTORS AND CONTROLLING SHAREHOLDERS

Despite the impression created by the collapse of Enron, Worldcom, and other corporations in the United States in 2002, corporate scandals involving dishonesty or carelessness by persons in charge of corporations are neither a new, nor a particularly United States, phenomena. Indeed, the collapse of the English South Sea Company in 1711 prompted the famous economist, Adam Smith, to question the viability of the joint stock company—what we now refer to as a business corporation—with its inevitable delegation of some persons to be in charge of "other peoples' money." This Chapter explores how laws in various nations seek to prevent mismanagement by those in charge of corporations.

SECTION A. DIRECTORS' CONDUCT

As discussed in Chapter IV, the worldwide model of corporate governance posits that corporations are managed by, or under the direction of, a board of directors. Yet, as mentioned above, the existence of corporate boards frequently seems accompanied by complaints about the directors' conduct. This section introduces a number of cases outside the United States in which complaints about director conduct resulted in judicial decisions. In reviewing these decisions, ask: (i) Are there common patterns to director misconduct regardless of where it occurs? (ii) Do judicial standards for minimally acceptable director conduct substantially converge or differ between various nations? (iii) What are appropriate remedies for director misconduct? (This Chapter will return to the third question in the final section.)

1. INATTENTION

INATTENTIVE DIRECTORS AND ROGUE TRADERS AT BARINGS AND DAIWA

based on Re Barings plc and others (No. 5) [1999] 1 BCLC 433 (Ch. Div. Companies Court); Nishimura v. Abekawa, 1721 Hanrei Jiho 3 (Osaka D. Ct., Sept. 20, 2000), translated in Bruce E. Aronson, *Learning from Comparative Law in Teaching U.S. Corporate Law: 1. Director's Liability in Japan and the U.S.*, 22 Penn St. Int'l L. Rev. 213 (2003).

In 1995, both England and Japan experienced remarkably similar corporate scandals involving major financial firms that suffered huge losses, in each case as a result of trading activities by one of the firms' middle managers. These losses led to legal actions against the directors of the English and Japanese firms in the courts of those countries.

The English scandal involved the venerable merchant bank, Barings plc., which had survived wars and depressions, but not the derivatives trading of Nick Leeson. Leeson was a manager and trader in a Singapore subsidiary of Barings. His trading purportedly involved arbitrage transactions in which he could take advantage of price differences for the same securities in different Asian markets by purchasing in the lower price market and, *at the same time*, selling in the higher price market— thus locking in a profit at little or no risk. In fact, however, Leeson's purchases and sales were not simultaneous, or, in some cases, even matched at all, meaning that Barings was exposed to the risk of price changes in the market while its position was open. As a result, instead of Leeson's trades producing income with little risk, they produced ever increasing losses. These losses dramatically escalated after the January 17, 1995 Kobe earthquake led to a significant increase in the volatility of Japanese financial markets. All told, Leeson's trades resulted in losses of £927 million, leading to the bankruptcy of Barings.

The Japanese scandal involved The Daiwa Bank Limited. A manager (named Toshihide Iguchi) in Daiwa's New York branch was in charge of the branch's securities custody department. In 1984, Iguchi's duties expanded from managing the custody department, to include trading in United States Treasury securities on Daiwa's behalf with the goal of making a profit for Daiwa from such trading. Instead of profits, Iguchi racked up losses. Apparently out of fear that reporting the losses would result in halting the new trading operation, and in the hope that he could recoup the losses, Iguchi engaged in unauthorized trades above the limit set by his superiors at Daiwa. This just resulted in more losses— such that, by the time (in July 1995) Iguchi confessed his misdeeds in a letter to Daiwa's president, Iguchi's eleven years of unauthorized trades had incurred $1.1 billion worth of losses for Daiwa. Compounding Daiwa's difficulties, its president and top executive directors, in violation of United States banking regulations, delayed notifying United States banking authorities about Iguchi's confession. As a result, United States banking regulators terminated Daiwa's ability to conduct banking operations in the United States and initiated a prosecution that led to Daiwa's paying a $340 million fine.

Naturally, in each case, the question arises as to how the trader (Leeson and Iguchi, respectively) was able to rack up such huge losses without his superiors in the company becoming aware of, and putting a stop to, the problem. The answer in both cases is similar: the trader had dual responsibilities. Leeson was in charge of both the trading activities (the so-called front office) at Barings' Singapore subsidiary, and, critically, also the paperwork involved in recording and settling the trades (the so-called back office). Being in charge of the paperwork allowed Leeson to manipulate the records so that they showed him making significant profits, when, in fact, he was incurring significant losses. In order to pay for the losses, Leeson requested funds from Barings in London purportedly to meet margin calls (which were actually bogus) on the accounts of Barings' clients. Along the same lines, Iguchi used the fact that he retained his position in charge of Daiwa's New York branch custody department to conceal the losses he incurred. Specifically, while Daiwa placed the actual custody of securities entrusted to its New York branch in the hands of a United States company, Bankers Trust—who would dispose of the securities in accordance with instructions it received from Daiwa and send account statements to Daiwa's New York branch—Iguchi's position as manager of the custody department enabled him to give such instructions and to receive the account statements. Accordingly, to obtain funds to cover the losses, Iguchi instructed Bankers Trust to sell securities held in custody for Daiwa and Daiwa's customers. Since Iguchi received the account statements from Bankers Trust, he was able to alter the statements before his superiors saw them, and thereby hide the sales and the misuse of the proceeds.

Both the Barings and Daiwa scandals led to legal actions against directors of the respective companies based upon the claim that the directors should have taken actions that would have led to the discovery and termination of Leeson's and Iguchi's trading activities before the losses had reached such staggering amounts. Here, however, there is an interesting divergence in the nature of the legal proceedings. The Daiwa proceeding will strike the student of corporate law in the United States as rather familiar: Daiwa shareholders brought a derivative action seeking damages for Daiwa against a large number of the company's past and present officers and directors. The shareholders claimed that these directors and officers had failed to carry out their duties with "the care of a good manager" and "faithfully on behalf of the company" as required under the Japanese Commercial Code. By contrast, the Barings action was brought by the English Secretary of State for Trade and Industry under the English Company Directors Disqualification Act of 1986. Section 6 of this Act calls for the court to issue an order disqualifying an individual from serving as a director of any company for a minimum of two and a maximum of fifteen years, when the court finds that the individual was a director of a company that has become insolvent, and that the individual's conduct as a director of the insolvent company "makes him unfit to be concerned in the management of a company."

In a lengthy opinion, an English chancery division court disqualified three individuals, who were directors of Barings or its subsidiaries, from serving as directors of any other company. (Seven other directors in the Barings group were also disqualified in less contested proceedings.) The court set out the applicable law as follows:

A. THE COURT'S JURISDICTION UNDER SECTION 6 OF THE ACT

* * *

The primary purpose of jurisdiction under s 6 is to protect the public against the future conduct of companies by persons whose past records as directors of insolvent companies have shown them to be a danger to others.

* * *

'Unfitness' may be shown by conduct which is dishonest * * * or by conduct which is merely incompetent.

* * *

Although in considering the question of unfitness the court must have regard (among other things) to any misfeasance or breach of any fiduciary or other duty by the respondent in relation to the company * * *, it is not in my judgment a prerequisite of a finding of unfitness that the respondent should have been guilty of misfeasance or breach of duty in relation to the company. * * * Conversely, in my judgment, the fact that a respondent may have been guilty of misfeasance or breach of duty does not necessarily mean that he is unfit. * * *

B. THE DUTIES OF DIRECTORS

* * *

In summary, the following general propositions can, in my judgment, be derived from the authorities to which I was referred in relation to the duties of directors:

(i) Directors have, both collectively and individually, a continuing duty to acquire and maintain a sufficient knowledge and understanding of the company's business to enable them properly to discharge their duties as directors.

(ii) Whilst directors are entitled * * * to delegate particular functions to those below them in the management chain, and to trust their competence and integrity to a reasonable extent, the exercise of the power of delegation does not absolve a director from the duty to supervise the discharge of the delegated functions.

(iii) No rule of universal application can be formulated as to the duty referred to in (ii) above. The extent of the duty, and the question whether it has been discharged, must depend on the facts of each particular case, including the director's role in the management of the company.

In holding that the three directors of Barings or its subsidiaries had breached their duties and demonstrated their unfitness, the court noted a number of failings that led to Leeson's activities going undetected. These included: (i) failure to implement the recommendation of an internal audit report to place Leeson's front office and back office roles in separate hands; (ii) failure to have the trading operation at the Singapore subsidiary independently reviewed in order to ensure risk limits were observed—despite this recommendation in an internal audit report, as well as the extraordinarily large percentage of Barings' revenues attributed to Leeson's activities, the existence of rumors in Asian markets about dangerously large positions held by Barings, and the continued disregard of directions to reduce the volume of Leeson's trading operation; and (iii) continued satisfying of Leeson's ever growing demands for funds purportedly to meet customer margin calls without any attempt to reconcile the amounts requested with the underlying positions—even in the face of Leeson's unsatisfactory explanations to Barings' outside auditors regarding a large year-end discrepancy between Leeson's records and externally generated statements of Barings' accounts.

The three directors involved in the case had management responsibilities that made, or, according to the court, should have made, them aware of these problems: One of the directors (Tuckey, who tried to defend his lack of monitoring by arguing that he acted primarily as a "rainmaker" dealing with investment banking clients) was the chairman of the management committee responsible for running Barings' overall investment banking operation; the second director (Baker) was the head of the financial products group—an organizational subdivision generally within the investment banking operation, which encompassed, among other activities, Leeson's trading; and the third director (Gamby) was the head of settlements (dealing with margin calls) for the investment banking operation. Of Mr. Tuckey, the director with the most distant relationship to Leeson's activities, the court wrote:

> Mr Tuckey's breaches of duty involved not so much discrete failures of management as a general failure to manage: they amount not so much to bad management as to *non*-management. * * * In particular, I regard it as seriously incompetent of Mr Tuckey [who admitted he did not fully understand the nature of Leeson's purported arbitrage] not to inform himself properly about the [the arbitrage] business [conducted by Leeson].

The shareholders derivative suit against the Daiwa directors and officers also produced a finding that three directors (who had been in charge of the New York branch during the relevant time) breached their duties; albeit there was only proof that one director's breach had caused damage. The Osaka District Court held this director liable for the trading losses Iguchi incurred for Daiwa during this director's tenure in charge of the New York branch (equaling $530 million). In reaching this result, the court explained:

> Conducting sound corporate management requires accurately assessing conditions of various kinds of risk which are produced in accordance with the type and nature of the business purpose, * * * and * * * establishing a risk management system (so-called internal control system) in response to the scale and nature, etc. of the business conducted by the corporation. Since the board of directors must pass a resolution for the performance of important business matters, the overall policy of a risk management system, which relates to the fundamentals of corporate management, requires the board of directors to pass a resolution. The representative director and director in charge (of a business department or function), who are in charge of business performance, bear the responsibility to decide specifically, based on the overall policy, the risk management system for the department(s) for which he is in charge. In this sense, directors, as members of the board of directors, and also as a representative director or director in charge, bear a duty to construct a risk management system, and, in addition, bear a duty to monitor whether or not the representative director and director in charge are performing their duty to establish a risk management system, and this also should be said to constitute the contents of the duty of care and duty of loyalty as a director.

* * *

> However, the contents of the risk management system to be created are gradually realized through the accumulation of experience in which risk materializes and causes various cases and incidents, and through progress on research concerning risk management. Accordingly, it would not be appropriate to take the level of risk management system which is currently required of financial institutions from the standpoint of ensuring sound and appropriate management of business in light of various financial scandals, and making it the decision standard in this case. Also, what should be the contents of the risk management system to be created is a question of business judgment, and we must be mindful that broad discretion is granted to directors who are specialists in corporate management.

Applying this standard—and despite what it had to say about the broad discretion of directors in matters of business judgment and the need for a court to avoid judgments based upon hindsight—the court found that the directors in charge of the New York branch were negligent in implementing internal controls, since they relied on the Bankers Life account statements sent through Iguchi (rather than confirmed directly from Bankers Life), thereby allowing Iguchi to hide his transactions.

One difference between the findings in the Barings and Daiwa proceedings is that the Japanese court exonerated most of the defendants charged with negligence in the failure to discover Iguchi's trades. To some extent, this might reflect nothing more than the broad sweep employed by the Daiwa shareholder plaintiffs in choosing whom to name as defendants, versus the more selective approach taken by the English Secretary of State for Trade and Industry. Still, this gave the Osaka District Court an opportunity to address when senior officers and directors will not be liable for misdeeds at lower levels:

> In a large-scale enterprise which has a vast structure like Daiwa Bank, having the president or the deputy president directly supervising each business (department or function) is, of course, inappropriate from the standpoint of efficient and rational management and is also not possible. With respect to confirmation of the custody account balances for U.S. treasuries, the Inspection Department and the New York Branch which are in charge of this have been established, and an organization has been created which anticipates that the directors in charge of both of these departments will, on their responsibility, conduct appropriate performance of their business. The president and deputy president are permitted to entrust the conduct of such business to each director in charge, and so long as there are no special circumstances which raise doubts about the contents of the business performance of each director in charge, it is reasonable to understand that [the president and deputy vice president] * * * will not bear liability for neglect of supervision of business. In this case, there are no allegations or proof of such special circumstances.

Similarly, the court found that the directors other than those involved with the New York branch were not negligent in establishing the overall risk management policy for Daiwa and in being unaware of the specific failings of the system of internal controls at New York.

Notes

1. In both *Daiwa* and *Barings*, the courts placed critical significance on the management responsibilities of the negligent individual board members, that were separate and apart from actions of the overall board. While, as mentioned in Chapter III, the basic concept of a board of directors is that the directors will make major corporate decisions by meeting together as peers, in Japan and other nations it is common for directors also to have individual management responsibilities. In fact, however, this is true in all nations whenever corporate executives also serve as members of the board of directors (so-called inside directors). The only real difference is that the inside director in the United States typically would have another title for his or her role as a corporate executive (e.g., "vice president") rather than carrying out individual management responsibilities under the title of "di-

rector." Hence, the findings of negligence in *Daiwa* and *Barings* involved persons acting in a role that United States terminology typically would have labeled that of executive or officer rather than director.

Given this clarification, compare the courts' approach to determining whether the directors (and officers) should have been aware of the rogue trading in *Daiwa* and *Barings*, with the approach of courts in classic cases in the United States, such as *Bates v. Dresser*, 251 U.S. 524 (1920) (holding a bank's president, but not its outside directors, negligent in failing to discover embezzlement by a bank employee). Are the similarities the result of linkages between the legal systems in England, the United States and Japan, or because the same factual issue—how much one can expect directors and superior officers in a corporation to be aware of misdeeds by employees— tends to lead to the same analysis? To what extent are there differences in the courts' approaches? Notice that the *Daiwa* opinion seems to be less willing than the *Barings* decision to find negligence by the defendants without a direct responsibility for the particular branch. Does this reflect different legal standards—or is this explicable by factual differences between the two situations, specifically, the numerous warning signs of major trouble in *Barings* (where Leeson's trading brought down the entire company within months), as opposed to the more subtle situation in *Daiwa* (where Iguchi's trading continued eleven years and may have continued even longer if Iguchi did not feel a need for confession)?

2. Compare who brought the derivative suit in *Daiwa* and the remedy the court imposed, with who brought the proceeding in *Barings* and the remedy imposed. What are the advantages and disadvantages of the different types of plaintiffs, and of the different types of remedies, as means to ensure directors pay attention to their jobs?

2. DECISIONS TO SUE MANAGERS AND OTHER DIRECTORS

ARAG/GARMENBECK CASE

BGHZ 135, 244 (Bundesgerichtshof [Federal Court of Justice], F.R.G. 1997). Translated in Andreas Cahn & David C. Donald, COMPARATIVE COMPANY LAW (forthcoming).

* * *

FACTS:

The Plaintiffs, members of the supervisory board of the Defendant, a liability insurer having the legal form of a stock corporation (*Aktiengesellschaft* [an AG]), challenge the supervisory board resolutions * * * [rejecting] a proposal to enforce a claim for damages against the Chairman of the management board of the Defendant, Dr. Ludwig F. * * *. [As an AG, German law required ARAG to have both a management board empowered to actually manage the company, and a supervisory board charged with supervising the management board. As Chairman of the management board, Ludwig F. was the company's CEO.]

The Defendant, [and] its 100% owned subsidiaries, * * * [pursuant to the actions] of their executive managers * * * , including Dr. Ludwig

F., entered into commercial dealings with G[armenbeck] Ltd. [Garmenbeck was an English company with little more than a post office box, that was run by an electrician who had a record of previous violations of law. As a result of Dr. Ludwig F's apparent gullibility in dealing with Garmenbeck, the Defendant and its subsidiaries fell victim to a pyramid scheme in which they lost over 80 million Deutsche Marks (around $60 million).]

* * *

The Plaintiffs argue that the Chairman of the Defendant's management board violated the duty of care that he owned his company by entering into the transactions with G[armenbeck] Ltd., and must therefore reimburse the company for the resulting damages. In its meetings of June 25, 1992 and June 15, 1993, the supervisory board adopted resolutions to reject the Plaintiffs' proposal that [the supervisory board prosecute a lawsuit on behalf of the Defendant company to recover damages from the Chairman of the Defendant's management board.]

The Plaintiffs argue that such resolutions are in violation of law and pray that the court declare them null and void.

The State Regional Court found merit in the complaint, but the Court of Appeals found that the complaint should be dismissed. We vacate the decision of the Court of Appeals and remand for further proceedings.

DISCUSSION:

[The court's discussion of the standing of the dissenting supervisory board members to bring this action is reprinted later in this Chapter.]

* * *

II. The Court of Appeals nevertheless incorrectly dismissed the claim.

* * *

1. [In dismissing the plaintiff's claim, the Court of Appeals reasoned as follows:] "The Court of Appeals initially grants the supervisory board a certain 'decision-making prerogative' in evaluating whether the damages action against the managing directors has a chance of success in court, and in so doing partially eliminates the court's ability to review the decision because of the prognostic element that any such decision contains. In addition, the supervisory board is supposed to receive additional discretionary freedom when performing its duties, thereby restraining the scope of judicial review—in a similar way as the restraint that must be exercised pursuant to § 114 of the Rules of Administrative Courts in administrative proceedings—in connection with the board's decisions made to fulfill tasks solely in the interest of the corporation. This includes a decision whether to prosecute a claim against a member of the management board for damages inflicted on the corporation. Such restraints on judicial review are advisable in order to avoid an overly

legalistic encasing of the work of the supervisory board, which includes supervision of not only the legality, but also the meaningfulness and commercial wisdom, of the management board's direction, and to leave the corporate management bodies a certain free space in which to exercise independent, business judgment. Such free discretion may be completely eliminated, thereby triggering a duty to take a specific action, only in exceptional cases, such as where the supervisory board's refusal to undertake a certain requested action is clearly illegal or where it would create substantial prejudice for the corporation, such as impairing corporate assets. In the case at hand, even without performing a detailed balancing test of the pros and cons of prosecuting the action against the management board Chairman, such a complete elimination of free discretion must be rejected. Neither an overreaching of discretion nor an abuse of discretion has been claimed by the Plaintiffs or is evident on the record."

2.   These reasons presented by the Court of Appeals may only be partially upheld on appeal.

a) The Court of Appeals is correct in finding that the supervisory board has the duty to take responsibility for discerning the existence of a damage claim of the corporation against its managing directors and as a body to examine the merits of the claim and prosecute it in accordance with law and the articles of association if the legal requirements for the prosecution of such claim exist. This duty arises both from the responsibility of the supervisory board to monitor the management activity of the management board (§ 111(1) AktG [the German marketable stock company statute]), which includes transactions that have already been concluded, and from the fact that the supervisory board represents the corporation in dealings with the management board both in and out of court (§ 112 AktG). * * *

b) However, the standards set out in the decision of the Court of Appeals that should guide the supervisory board's examination and decision are either ambiguous or inapplicable.

aa) A supervisory board decision on whether a managing director should be sued for damages for violating his management duties first of all requires a determination of whether facts exist that create a liability for damages pursuant to law and an analysis of the procedural risks and merits of the claim. When deciding whether a given fact pattern justifies a claim that the management board has acted culpably and violated its duties, the supervisory board must take into account that, in directing the corporation's business, the management board must be given the wide range of free discretion that is essential for the operation of a business. In addition to consciously running business risks, this generally also includes the danger of bad decisions and incorrect evaluations, to which every businessman—regardless of how responsible—is subject. If the supervisory board receives the impression that the management board lacks the necessary good sense for the successful management of the company, that is, it just does not have the "right touch" in performing its management functions, this may lead the supervisory board to seek the removal of the relevant managing directors. This does not lead to a claim for compensation of damages. Such a claim may be raised only when a manager goes significantly beyond the limits of a business judgment characterized by responsible management oriented solely towards the good of the corporation and based on a careful evaluation of the relevant facts, i.e., where the readiness to engage in business risks is irresponsibly breached, or the comportment of the management board is otherwise in breach of duty.

bb) Contrary to the opinion of the Court of Appeals, the supervisory board may not invoke a "decision-making prerogative" to restrict the scope of the court's review with regard to this part of its decision-making. In examining whether a claim for damages exists and the merits thereof, the supervisory board does nothing other than anyone else who evaluates—for himself or for another—whether a claim exists and whether it may be successfully prosecuted in court. The substance and correctness of such an evaluation of the merits of judicial prosecution of a claim may, in cases of a dispute, generally be fully tested in a court, given that such an evaluation does not regard business dealings but rather solely regards an area of knowledge for which we may always consider positing a limited freedom for discretion. Questions entail business judgment only if the decision concerns a choice between various business alternatives.

cc) If the supervisory board performs such a thorough and appropriate procedural risk assessment and concludes that the corporation probably—in these circumstances, certainty cannot be required—has a claim for damages against one of its managing directors, the question may be asked at the next step * * * whether the supervisory board may in any case refrain from prosecuting the claim and with it the compensation of the corporation for damages suffered.

Contrary to the opinion of the Court of Appeals, in making this decision the supervisory board has no free space for autonomous discretion. Freedom of business judgment is a part and a necessary complement given to the management duties of the management board, but not to those of the supervisory board. The supervisory board shares in such freedom only where the law gives it business-related tasks, such as in appointing and removing the members of the management board, * * * i.e., above all in all those areas where the supervisory board must accompany the management board's business activities with prospective examination. Decisions regarding prosecuting damages claims against a managing director's breach of duty are, rather, a part of its retrospective supervisory activity, which is designed to ensure that the management board fulfills its duties and to avoid damage to the corporation. * * * Since this decision must be guided solely by the good of the corporation, which generally requires that any damage to the assets of the corporation be compensated, the supervisory board may refrain from prosecuting an apparently well-grounded claim for damages against a management board that has breached its duties only in those exceptional cases in which important interests and needs of the corporation argue that the damage should be suffered without compensation. Such requirement will as a rule only be met if the interests and needs of the corporation that seem to argue against compensating the corporation for the damage caused by the management board outweigh, or at least roughly equal, the considerations that argue for prosecution. In this regard, the considerations raised by the Court of Appeals, such as a negative impact on the business activity, the public reputation of the corporation, impairment of the management board's productivity, and damage to the business climate may certainly be meaningful. On the other hand, the supervisory board may give weight to considerations other than the good of the corporation, such as protecting a deserving management board member or the potential social consequences of the prosecution for the board member and his family, only in exception cases. Such an exceptional case could be, for example, where the breach of duty is insubstantial and the damage suffered by the corporation is relatively slight, but the foreseeable consequences for the board member who would be liable for compensation are quite threatening.

c) The analysis set forth above leads to the conclusion that damages claims against managing directors must, as a rule, be prosecuted. Only very important countervailing reasons and a special justification will support not prosecuting a claim that has a probability of success—which would closely resemble the corporation itself waiving the claim—and thus must be an exceptional case.

Only within these narrow limits may, following the approach of the Court of Appeals, the supervisory board be granted discretionary freedom in deciding whether, in exceptional cases, to refrain from prosecuting a damages claim, in spite of its chances of success, because of very important considerations regarding the good of the corporation. However, such discretionary freedom of the supervisory board may only apply after the counterbalancing circumstances have been established.

III. Because its legal approach deviated from our own, the Court of Appeals failed to make any findings as to whether the Chairman of the Defendant's management board is in fact subject to a claim for damages that has a likelihood of success on the merits. There also have been no findings as to whether there are important considerations regarding the good of the corporation that allow the supervisory board, as an exceptional case, to exercise its discretion in deciding whether to refrain from prosecuting the claim. The Court of Appeals also failed to perform a detailed evaluation and balancing of the considerations for and against prosecuting the claim against the Chairman of the management board. The appealed decision is hereby overruled and the matter is therefore remanded back to the Court of Appeals for a re-examination and decision.

Notes

1. Examine the court's discussion of how the supervisory board is to evaluate whether to bring an action against members of the management board—specifically, the explanation that a claim exists "only when a manager goes significantly beyond the limits of a business judgment characterized by responsible management oriented solely towards the good of the corporation and based upon a careful evaluation of the relevant facts." How does this compare with the business judgment rule as expressed by courts in the United States? How does it compare with the following standard of review described by the Tokyo District Court in a derivative suit involving Nomura Securities:

> Suppose a case raises the propriety of a director's business judgment. The reasonable approach for a court is not to decide at the outset what the director should have done, and then to compare that decision with the judgment the director actually made. Rather, the court should first examine the business judgment the director made. Then, it should ask whether the director either (i) made a careless error in assessing the factual premises to that judgment, or (ii) in making the judgment used a process that for an ordinary business executive would have been egregiously unreasonable.

Ikenaga v Tabuchi, 1469 Hanrei Jiho 25 (Tokyo D. Ct., Sept. 16, 1993), translated in J. Mark Ramseyer & Minoru Nakazato, JAPANESE LAW: AN ECONOMIC APPROACH 112–113 (1999).

In 2005, the German legislature amended the law governing the marketable stock company (an AG) to codify a business judgment rule:

> There will be no breach of duty when a member of the management board, in making a business decision, could reasonably assume, on the basis of appropriate information, that the member was acting in the interest of the corporation. Aktiengesetz § 93(1).

How does this compare with the standard expressed by the court in *Garmenbeck* for evaluating the conduct of members of the managing board? How does it compare with the business judgment rule in the United States? Interestingly enough, the German statute contains a provision making directors liable only in the event they are grossly negligent—but this applies just when individual creditors assert the corporation's claim against directors. One other twist in German law, as compared with the business judgment rule in the United States, is that the directors bear the burden of proof on the issue of due care. *Id.* at (2), (5).

Why do courts in the United States and other countries feel it necessary to remind themselves of the need to exercise restraint in second guessing the business decisions of directors? Do courts in the United States or other countries exercise the same restraint in second guessing the judgment of doctors or others accused of breaching their duty of care?

2. Why was court less deferential to the supervisory board when it came to deciding if the corporation should sue members of the management board then the court would have been if the matter had involved some other

purely business decision? In focusing on the fact that the likelihood of successful litigation is not a matter of *business* expertise, did the court overlook another concern? How will a court decide if the merits of a case make it worthwhile for the corporation to sue a manager or director? If the court must conduct a trial on the merits in order to determine whether the suit is worth bringing, do you see a practical problem with the end result in situations in which the court concludes, after such a trial, that the suit was a bad idea?

3. ILLEGAL CORPORATE CONDUCT

DIRECTORS AND ILLEGAL CONDUCT AT HAZAMA AND DAIWA

based on Matsumaru v. Ootsuru, 15 Hanrei Jiho 3 (Tokyo D. Ct., Dec. 22, 1994), translated in J. Mark Ramseyer & Minoru Nakazato, JAPANESE LAW: AN ECONOMIC APPROACH 112–113 (1999); Nishimura v. Abekawa, 1721 Hanrei Jiho 3 (Osaka D. Ct., Sept. 20, 2000), translated in Bruce E. Aronson, *Learning from Comparative Law in Teaching U.S. Corporate Law: 1. Director's Liability in Japan and the U.S.*, 22 Penn St. Int'l L. Rev. 213 (2003).

In a pair of noted cases decided within the last dozen years, Japanese courts dealt with derivative suits brought against directors who had their corporations engage in illegal conduct.

In 1994, the Tokyo District Court dealt with a derivative suit brought against a director of Hazama-gumi Ltd. (a construction company), who bribed the mayor of a town in order to obtain the contract to build the town's new gymnasium. The court held the director had to repay Hazama the amount of the bribe. The court explained:

> Obviously, in doing business, companies may not use strongly anti-social tactics like bribery that violate the Criminal Code. They may not justify bribery as a business strategy on the grounds either (i) that it raises corporate profits, or (ii) that because their competitors customarily bribe they could not otherwise obtain business.

Six years later, the Osaka District Court issued the ruling in the *Daiwa* case discussed previously in this Chapter. The previous discussion of the *Daiwa* case focused on the claims that the defendant officers and directors of Daiwa Bank breached their duty to Daiwa in failing to detect and prevent unauthorized trades of a manager in Daiwa's New York branch before the losses Daiwa suffered from these trades reached $1.1 billion. As mentioned in the previous discussion, to add to the injury, the decision of Daiwa's senior officers and directors to delay reporting the manager's transgressions to United States' banking officials, as required by United States' banking regulations, resulted in Daiwa paying a $340 million fine and losing permission to conduct banking business in the United States. Interestingly, upon learning of the unauthorized trading, Daiwa's senior management had consulted with officials of the Japanese government's Ministry of Finance (MOF) for advice on how to react. In what turned out to be bad advice, the MOF officials encouraged delay in disclosing what had occurred, apparently fearing the impact of immediate disclosure on confidence in the Japanese banking system. The sanctions Daiwa incurred as a result of following this advice led to an additional derivative claim by Daiwa shareholders against Daiwa's directors and officers. The Osaka District Court held that the Daiwa officers and directors who approved the delay were liable to reimburse the corporation for the resulting fine:

> [E]ven assuming they did not sufficiently understand the detailed contents of U.S. banking laws, an incident in which one suffers a large loss of some 1.1 billion dollars due to unauthorized trading and unauthorized sales * * * should have prompted an immediate investigation and examination of U.S. laws relating to such a rare and unusual case. * * *

> [T]o pursue liability against a director for a past management measure as a violation of the duty of care and duty of loyalty requires that, at the time the business measure was taken, there was an important and careless mistake in grasping the facts which form the basis of the director's judgment or the process, [and/or] substance of decision-making was especially unreasonable or inappropriate as a business manager. However, although directors are granted broad discretion, in conducting corporate management they are required to comply with laws and ordinances, including foreign law * * * and * * * are not granted discretion about whether or not to comply with laws and ordinances, including foreign laws. * * * Even considering the difficult situation of Daiwa Bank at the time, [the defendants] made an extremely unreasonable and inappropriate business judgment as corporate business managers in violation of directors' duties of care and loyalty.

> Defendants in the Violation of Law Case argue that there was no possibility (*kitai kanosei*) of going against the requests and suggestions of the Ministry of Finance (MOF) and reporting to U.S. authorities the facts of the unauthorized trading and unauthorized sales in this case. However, there is not sufficient evidence submitted to this court to find that MOF, based on its authority, gave defendants Akira Fujita et. al. instructions or orders that they not report to U.S. authorities. Rather, as long as Daiwa Bank conducted banking business in the United States, they had an obligation to observe United States' laws and regulations affecting banks. As managers of a bank, defendants Akira Fujita et. al. were responsible for making appropriate business judgments on their own. Even though the Japanese economy has developed and expanded on a global scale, defendants Akira Fujita et. al. adhered to informal local rules which are accepted only in Japan. The defendants sought to overcome Daiwa Bank's crisis by relying on the prestige of the Director General of MOF's Banking Bureau. As a result, they suffered harsh treatment from United States authorities. The argument of the defendants in the Violation of Law Case that there was no possibility (*kitai kanosei*) means that it is permissible to conduct banking business by relying on the decisions and instructions of the

MOF without making decisions based on their own judgment and at their own responsibility. We naturally reject such an argument.

Note

Compare these Japanese court decisions with *Miller v. A.T. & T. Co.*, 507 F.2d 759 (3rd Cir. 1974) (directors will be liable to the corporation if they had the corporation make an illegal campaign contribution). One added wrinkle when dealing with global enterprises such as Daiwa Bank is the possibility of inconsistent legal regulation. Should the Osaka District Court have shown greater sympathy for the defendant's argument that Japanese government officials from the MOF had encouraged the bank to delay disclosure to United States' regulators?

4.   DECISIONS IMPACTING OTHER STAKEHOLDERS

RE PEOPLE'S DEPARTMENT STORES LTD (1992) INC.

[2004] 3 S.C.R. 461 (Supreme Court of Canada, 2004).

I. Introduction

The principal question raised by this appeal is whether directors of a corporation owe a fiduciary duty to the corporation's creditors comparable to the statutory duty owed to the corporation. For the reasons that follow, we conclude that directors owe a duty of care to creditors, but that duty does not rise to a fiduciary duty. * * *

As a result of the demise in the mid–1990s of two major retail chains in eastern Canada, Wise Stores Inc. ("Wise") and its wholly-owned subsidiary, Peoples Department Stores Inc. ("Peoples"), the indebtedness of a number of Peoples' [trade] creditors went unsatisfied. In the wake of the failure of the two chains, Caron Bélanger Ernst & Young Inc., Peoples' trustee in bankruptcy (the "trustee"), brought an action against the directors of Peoples. To address the trustee's claims, the extent of the duties imposed by s. 122(1) of the *Canada Business Corporations Act* ("CBCA") upon directors with respect to creditors must be determined.

* * *

II. Background

Wise was founded by Alex Wise in 1930 as a small clothing store on St–Hubert Street in Montreal. By 1992, through expansion effected by a mix of internal growth and acquisitions, it had become an enterprise operating at 50 locations with annual sales of approximately $100 million, and it had been listed on the Montreal Stock Exchange in 1986. The stores were, for the most part, located in urban areas in Quebec. The founder's three sons, Lionel, Ralph and Harold Wise (the "Wise brothers"), were majority shareholders, officers, and directors of Wise. Together, they controlled 75 percent of the firm's equity.

In 1992, Peoples had been in business continuously in one form or another for 78 years. It had operated as an unincorporated division of Marks & Spencer Canada Inc. ("M & S") until 1991 [when M & S incorporated Peoples with the plan of selling the company]* * *. Peoples' 81 stores were generally located in rural areas, from Ontario to Newfoundland. Peoples had annual sales of about $160 million, but was struggling financially. Its annual losses were in the neighbourhood of $10 million.

[In 1992, Wise bought Peoples from M & S in a leveraged buy-out. As a result] Peoples became a subsidiary directly owned and controlled by Wise. The three Wise brothers were Peoples' only directors.

Following the acquisition, Wise had attempted to rationalize its operations by consolidating the overlapping corporate functions of Wise and Peoples, and operating as a group.* * * Almost from the outset, the joint operation of Wise and Peoples did not function smoothly. Instead of the expected synergies, the consolidation resulted in dissonance.

* * *

Before long, the parallel bookkeeping combined with the shared warehousing arrangements caused serious problems for both Wise and Peoples. The actual situation in the warehouse often did not mirror the reported state of the inventory in the system. The goods of one company were often inextricably commingled and confused with the goods of the other. As a result, the inventory records of both companies were increasingly incorrect. A physical inventory count was conducted to try to rectify the situation, to little avail. Both Wise and Peoples stores experienced numerous shipping disruptions and delays. The situation, already unsustainable, was worsening.

In October 1993, Lionel Wise consulted David Clément, Wise's (and, after the acquisition, Peoples') vice-president of administration and finance, in an attempt to find a solution. In January 1994, Clément recommended and the three Wise brothers agreed that they would implement a joint inventory procurement policy (the "new policy") whereby the two firms would divide responsibility for purchasing. Peoples would make all purchases from North American suppliers and Wise would, in turn, make all purchases from overseas suppliers. Peoples would then transfer to Wise what it had purchased for Wise, charging Wise accordingly, and vice versa. The new policy was implemented on February 1, 1994. It was this arrangement that was later criticized by certain creditors and by the trial judge.

Approximately 82 percent of the total inventory of Wise and Peoples was purchased from North American suppliers, which inevitably meant that Peoples would be extending a significant trade credit to Wise.

* * *

In December 1994, three days after the Wise brothers presented financial statements showing disappointing results for Peoples in its third fiscal quarter, M & S [to whom Peoples and Wise owed money as a result of the leveraged buyout] initiated bankruptcy proceedings against both Wise and Peoples.

* * *

Following the bankruptcy, Peoples' trustee filed a petition against the Wise brothers. In the petition, the trustee claimed that they had favoured the interests of Wise over Peoples to the detriment of Peoples' creditors, in breach of their duties as directors under s. 122(1) of the CBCA.

* * *

The trial judge, Greenberg J., relying on decisions from the United Kingdom, Australia and New Zealand, held that the fiduciary duty and the duty of care under s. 122 (1) of the CBCA extend to a company's creditors when a company is insolvent or in the vicinity of insolvency. Greenberg J. found that the implementation, by the Wise brothers qua directors of Peoples, of a corporate policy that affected both companies, had occurred while the corporation was in the vicinity of insolvency and was detrimental to the interests of the creditors of Peoples. The Wise brothers were therefore found liable and the trustee was awarded $4.44 million in damages. * * * All the parties appealed.

The Quebec Court of Appeal, * * * allowed the appeals by * * * the Wise brothers.

* * *

III. Analysis

At the outset, it should be acknowledged that according to art. 300 of the C.C.Q. [*Civil Code of Québec*] and s. 8.1 of the *Interpretation Act*, the civil law serves as a supplementary source of law to federal legislation such as the CBCA. Since the CBCA does not entitle creditors to sue directors directly for breach of their duties, it is appropriate to have recourse to the *Civil Code of Québec* to determine how rights grounded in a federal statute should be addressed in Quebec, and more specifically how s. 122(1) of the CBCA can be harmonized with the principles of civil liability.

This case came before our Court on the issue of whether directors owe a duty to creditors. The creditors did not bring a derivative action or an oppression remedy application under the CBCA. Instead, the trustee, representing the interests of the creditors, sued the directors for an alleged breach of the duties imposed by s. 122(1) of the CBCA. The standing of the trustee to sue was not questioned.

* * *

Subsection 122(1) of the CBCA establishes two distinct duties to be discharged by directors and officers in managing, or supervising the management of, the corporation:

122. (1) Every director and officer of a corporation in exercising their powers and discharging their duties shall

> (a) act honestly and in good faith with a view to the best interests of the corporation; and

> (b) exercise the care, diligence and skill that a reasonably prudent person would exercise in comparable circumstances.

The first duty has been referred to in this case as the "fiduciary duty". It is better described as the "duty of loyalty". We will use the expression "statutory fiduciary duty" for purposes of clarity when referring to the duty under the CBCA. This duty requires directors and officers to act honestly and in good faith with a view to the best interests of the corporation. The second duty is commonly referred to as the "duty of care". Generally speaking, it imposes a legal obligation upon directors and officers to be diligent in supervising and managing the corporation's affairs.

The trial judge did not apply or consider separately the two duties imposed on directors by s. 122(1). * * * They are, in fact, distinct and are designed to secure different ends. For that reason, they will be addressed separately in these reasons.

A. *The Statutory Fiduciary Duty: Section 122(1)(a) of the CBCA*

* * *

In our opinion, the trial judge's determination that there was no fraud or dishonesty in the Wise brothers' attempts to solve the mounting inventory problems of Peoples and Wise stands in the way of a finding that they breached their fiduciary duty. Greenberg J. stated, at para. 180:

> We hasten to add that in the present case, the Wise Brothers derived no direct personal benefit from the new domestic inventory procurement policy, albeit that, as the controlling shareholders of Wise Stores, there was an indirect benefit to them. Moreover, as was conceded by the other parties herein, in deciding to implement the new domestic inventory procurement policy, there was no dishonesty or fraud on their part.

* * *

As explained above, there is no doubt that both Peoples and Wise were struggling with a serious inventory management problem. The Wise brothers considered the problem and implemented a policy they hoped would solve it. In the absence of evidence of a personal interest or improper purpose in the new policy, and in light of the evidence of a desire to make both Wise and Peoples "better" corporations, we find that the directors did not breach their fiduciary duty under s. 122(1)(*a*) of the CBCA.

* * * Insofar as the statutory fiduciary duty [under the CBCA] is concerned, it is clear that the phrase the "best interests of the corporation" should be read not simply as the "best interests of the sharehold-

ers". From an economic perspective, the "best interests of the corporation" means the maximization of the value of the corporation. However, the courts have long recognized that various other factors may be relevant in determining what directors should consider in soundly managing with a view to the best interests of the corporation. For example, in *Teck Corp. v. Millar* (1972), 33 D.L.R. (3d) 288 (B.C. S.C.), Berger J. stated, at p. 314:

> A classical theory that once was unchallengeable must yield to the facts of modern life. * * * If today the directors of a company were to consider the interests of its employees no one would argue that in doing so they were not acting *bona fide* in the interests of the company itself. Similarly, if the directors were to consider the consequences to the community of any policy that the company intended to pursue, * * * it could not be said that they had not considered bona fide the interests of the shareholders.

> I appreciate that it would be a breach of their duty for directors to disregard entirely the interests of a company's shareholders in order to confer a benefit on its employees. But if they observe a decent respect for other interests lying beyond those of the company's shareholders in the strict sense, that will not, in my view, leave directors open to the charge that they have failed in their fiduciary duty to the company.

* * * We accept as an accurate statement of law that in determining whether they are acting with a view to the best interests of the corporation it may be legitimate, given all the circumstances of a given case, for the board of directors to consider, inter alia, the interests of shareholders, employees, suppliers, creditors, consumers, governments and the environment.

The various shifts in interests that naturally occur as a corporation's fortunes rise and fall do not, however, affect the content of the fiduciary duty under s. 122(1)(*a*) of the CBCA. At all times, directors and officers owe their fiduciary obligation to the corporation. The interests of the corporation are not to be confused with the interests of the creditors or those of any other stakeholders.

The interests of shareholders, those of the creditors and those of the corporation may and will be consistent with each other if the corporation is profitable and well capitalized and has strong prospects. However, this can change if the corporation starts to struggle financially. The residual rights of the shareholders will generally become worthless if a corporation is declared bankrupt. * * *

Short of bankruptcy, as the corporation approaches what has been described as the "vicinity of insolvency", the residual claims of shareholders will be nearly exhausted. While shareholders might well prefer that the directors pursue high-risk alternatives with a high potential payoff to maximize the shareholders' expected residual claim, creditors in the same circumstances might prefer that the directors steer a safer course so as to maximize the value of their claims against the assets of the corporation.

The directors' fiduciary duty does not change when a corporation is in the nebulous "vicinity of insolvency". That phrase has not been defined; moreover, it is incapable of definition and has no legal meaning. * * *

* * * In resolving these competing interests, it is incumbent upon the directors to act honestly and in good faith with a view to the best interests of the corporation. In using their skills for the benefit of the corporation when it is in troubled waters financially, the directors must be careful to attempt to act in its best interests by creating a "better" corporation, and not to favour the interests of any one group of stakeholders. If the stakeholders cannot avail themselves of the statutory fiduciary duty (the duty of loyalty, *supra*) to sue the directors for failing to take care of their interests, they have other means at their disposal.

The Canadian legal landscape with respect to stakeholders is unique. Creditors are only one set of stakeholders, but their interests are protected in a number of ways. * * * The oppression remedy of s. 241(2)(c) of the CBCA and the similar provisions of provincial legislation regarding corporations grant the broadest rights to creditors of any common law jurisdiction.

* * *

Section 241(2)(c) authorizes a court to grant a remedy if the powers of the directors of the corporation or any of its affiliates are or have been exercised in a manner that is oppressive or unfairly prejudicial to or that unfairly disregards the interests of any security holder, creditor, director or officer.

* * *

Section 241 of the CBCA provides a possible mechanism for creditors to protect their interests from the prejudicial conduct of directors. In our view, the availability of such a broad oppression remedy undermines any perceived need to extend the fiduciary duty imposed on directors by s. 122(1)(a) of the CBCA to include creditors.

* * *

B.   The Statutory Duty of Care: Section 122(1)(b) of the CBCA

As mentioned above, the CBCA does not provide for a direct remedy for creditors against directors for breach of their duties and the C.C.Q. is used as suppletive law.

* * *

To determine the applicability of extra-contractual liability in this appeal, it is necessary to refer to art. 1457 of the C.C.Q.:

> Every person has a duty to abide by the rules of conduct which lie upon him, according to the circumstances, usage or law, so as not to cause injury to another.

Where he is endowed with reason and fails in this duty, he is responsible for any injury he causes to another person by such fault and is liable to reparation for the injury, whether it be bodily, moral or material in nature.

* * *

Three elements of art. 1457 of the C.C.Q. are relevant to the integration of the director's duty of care into the principles of extra-contractual liability: who has the duty ("every person"), to whom is the duty owed ("another") and what breach will trigger liability ("rules of conduct"). It is clear that directors and officers come within the expression "every person". It is equally clear that the word "another" can include the creditors.

* * *

The first paragraph of art. 1457 does not set the standard of conduct. Instead, it incorporates by reference s. 122(1)(*b*) of the CBCA. The statutory duty of care is a "duty to abide by [a rule] of conduct which lie[s] upon [them], according to the ... law, so as not to cause injury to another".

* * *

Canadian courts, like their counterparts in the United States, the United Kingdom, Australia and New Zealand, * * * have developed a rule of deference to business decisions called the "business judgment rule", adopting the American name for the rule.

* * *

Directors and officers will not be held to be in breach of the duty of care under s. 122(1)(*b*) of the CBCA if they act prudently and on a reasonably informed basis. The decisions they make must be reasonable business decisions in light of all the circumstances about which the directors or officers knew or ought to have known. In determining whether directors have acted in a manner that breached the duty of care, it is worth repeating that perfection is not demanded. Courts are ill-suited and should be reluctant to second-guess the application of business expertise to the considerations that are involved in corporate decision making, but they are capable, on the facts of any case, of determining whether an appropriate degree of prudence and diligence was brought to bear in reaching what is claimed to be a reasonable business decision at the time it was made.

The trustee alleges that the Wise brothers breached their duty of care under s. 122(1)(*b*) of the CBCA by implementing the new procurement policy to the detriment of Peoples' creditors. After considering all the evidence, we agree with the Court of Appeal that the implementation of the new policy was a reasonable business decision that was made with a view to rectifying a serious and urgent business problem in circumstances in which no solution may have been possible. The trial judge's conclusion that the new policy led inexorably to Peoples' failure and bankruptcy was factually incorrect and constituted a palpable and overriding error.

In fact, * * * there were many factors other than the new policy that contributed more directly to Peoples' bankruptcy. Peoples had lost $10 million annually while being operated by M & S. * * * Unfortunately for both Wise and Peoples, the retail market in eastern Canada had become very competitive in the early 1990s, and this trend continued with the arrival of Wal–Mart in 1994.

* * *

Notes

1. Why did it matter whether or not directors of a Canadian corporation owe a fiduciary duty (i.e. a duty of loyalty), rather than just a duty of care, to creditors—particularly since the court found that the Wise brothers did not act for personal gain or an improper purpose, but rather to make a better corporation, and therefore did not breach their fiduciary duty?

Suppose a corporation is in the vicinity of insolvency (its assets barely exceed its debts). Presumably, if the corporation immediately winds up, the creditors will get fully paid; if the company continues, any losses create the risk that the creditors will not be fully paid, but any gains (above some fixed rate of interest) will go to the shareholders. Under these circumstances, if the company's prospects present a significant risk of failure so that it would be in the creditors' interest to wind things up, would a duty of loyalty to the creditors compel liquidation of the company? What difference if there is only a duty of care toward creditors? What would a duty of loyalty to the corporation demand? Does the court's holding produce the socially optimal result?

To apply the court's holding to a different situation, notice that Wise Stores, Inc. bought Peoples Department Stores, Inc. in what is known as a leveraged buy-out—in other words, Peoples ended up on the hook for the debt incurred to M & S to buy Peoples from M & S. The result of this added debt is to place Peoples in greater risk of bankruptcy and to make all other debt of Peoples riskier. The trustee did not challenge the leveraged buy-out. Suppose, however—contra to the actual facts of the case—that Peoples had issued bonds (tradeable debt instruments) before the leveraged buy-out. The market price of such bonds depends upon their riskiness—meaning that a leveraged buy-out will cause the market price of outstanding bonds to decline. At the same time, the debt incurred in a leveraged buy-out goes to pay the former shareholders for their stock. Hence, even without a bankruptcy, the bondholders (creditors), who have lost market value for their investment so that shareholders can get money, might seek to challenge the leveraged buy-out. *Metropolitan Life Ins. Co. v. RJR Nabisco, Inc.*, 716 F. Supp. 1504 (S.D.N.Y. 1989). In this situation, is there some significance to whether the directors owe creditors a duty of loyalty, a duty of care, or no extra-contractual duty at all? Does the court's test that the duty of loyalty calls for making a better corporation provide an optimal answer to whether directors breached their duty of loyalty by approving this leveraged buy-out? How would one apply a duty of care toward creditors to this situation?

2. The standing of a bankruptcy trustee to assert actions against corporate directors for the ultimate benefit of the corporation's unpaid creditors is widely recognized in common law jurisdictions (e.g., Insolvency Act, 1986, c. 45, § 165 (Eng.))—including the United States—as well as civil law jurisdictions (e.g., Insolvenzordung [Insolvency Code] §§ 80, 148(1) (F.R.G.)). Why then does the court assert that Canada grants creditors of corporations the broadest right of any common law jurisdiction? What are the advantages and disadvantages of creating a judicial remedy available for creditors, who claim that actions by the directors are oppressive? More broadly, what are the advantages and disadvantages of extending standing to creditors as a mechanism for holding directors accountable?

3. What about other stakeholders in the corporation, such as employees or the community? The court states that directors will not breach their duty to shareholders by taking into account the interests of employees or the community. Is this consistent with cases in the United States? Even if the bottom line is the same, does the Canadian court feel the need to rationalize looking out for the employees, or for the community's welfare, as being somehow in the long-range interest of the shareholders?

Moving beyond whether directors *may* look out for the interests of employees, the community or other stakeholders, *must* directors look out for such interests under corporate law in the United States? In Canada? In other nations? Consider the law in the Netherlands. Under Article 26 of the Netherlands Enterprise Councils Act, works councils can challenge decisions by a Dutch corporation's management before a specialized court in Amsterdam. The court is empowered to block implementation of the decision if the "entrepreneur in balancing the interests involved, could not reasonably have come to his decision." The court has applied this standard to block corporations from closing down divisions and profitable (and even unprofitable) subsidiaries in the Netherlands. *E.g.*, Eddy Wymeersch, *A Status Report on Corporate Governance in Some Continental European States*, in COMPARATIVE CORPORATE GOVERNANCE—THE STATE OF THE ART AND EMERGING RESEARCH 1082 (1998) (Klaus J. Hopt, et. al. eds.); Winfried van den Muijsenbergh, *Corporate Governance: The Dutch Experience*, 16 Transnat'l L. 63, 69–70 (2002). Commonly, in these cases, the court's objection to the decision's reasonableness stems not from the decision's substantive merits, as much as from the process that management utilized in making the decision—for example, whether the management had explored other alternatives. Compare this focus on process with the application of a business judgment rule in the United States and in other nations. Regardless of whether the focus is on substance or just process, should stakeholders, such as employees, of corporations within the United States be able to sue directors who make decisions for the corporation contrary to the employees' (or other stakeholders') interest?

4. Notice the court's blending of a provincial (Quebec) civil law rule with a national corporation statute. Is the blending of civil and common law, and national and sub-national law, unique to Canadian corporate law?

5. EXECUTIVE COMPENSATION

MANNESMANN CASE

Case No. 3 StR 470/04 (Bundesgerichtshof [Federal Court of Justice], F.R.G. 2005).
Translations of portions of the opinion by Alexander Klauser, Klaus Linke, Katherina Pistor and David Donald.

[Facts:

This is an appeal from an acquittal by the trial court in a criminal prosecution brought against members of the supervisory board of Mannesmann AG, who voted to award a large bonus to the departing CEO of the company following a takeover.

Mannesmann AG was a German marketable stock company. While Mannesmann traditionally had produced heavy machinery and the like, starting in 1990, Mannesmann became increasingly focused on operating a cell phone network (creating Germany's first cell phone network in partnership with AirTouch). In the 1990s, Mannesmann expanded its cell phone activities beyond Germany through a program of increasing its holdings in other cell phone companies. Klaus Esser, Mannesmann's Chief Financial Officer at the time, was instrumental in this program. In May 1999, Esser became Mannesmann's CEO. Esser successfully continued Mannesmann's expansion by acquiring other cell phone companies.

In November 1999, a British cell phone company, Vodafone plc—having just acquired AirTouch—launched an effort to take over Mannesmann. After Esser rejected a friendly offer from Vodafone's CEO—under which Mannesmann stockholders would have received stock in Vodafone with a market value of 203 euros for each surrendered share of Mannesmann—Vodafone made a hostile tender offer at 240 euros per share. Esser and Mannesmann's board urged Mannesmann's stockholders to reject the bid as inadequate. When it eventually became clear, however, that a majority of Mannesmann's stockholders wanted to take the Vodafone offer, Esser yielded and negotiated a friendly takeover. The final deal, reached on February 3, 2000, valued Mannesmann stock at 360 euros per share—thereby gaining Mannesmann stockholders a total of 63 billion euros more in Vodafone stock than the original offer rejected by Esser. With respect to Esser himself, under the deal he would not, except for a short transitional period, continue to run Mannesmann, but, instead, would resign from Mannesmann's management board effective July 31, 2000.

As a German AG, Mannesmann had both a management board to run the company, and a supervisory board to supervise the management board—including setting compensation for members of the management board. Because Mannesmann had over 20,000 employees in Germany, German law required the supervisory board to have 20 members—half elected by employees and half by the stockholders.

One of the members elected by the stockholders to Mannesmann's supervisory board (Mr. Fok) was a managing director of a Hong Kong company that had become the largest stockholder in Mannesmann by virtue of one of Mannesmann's cell phone company acquisitions. Fok felt that Esser's existing compensation plan did not provide adequate recognition of Esser's extraordinary contributions to increasing the price of Mannesmann stock—both before and during the takeover contest— especially in light of the fact that the Mannesmann compensation package, unlike compensation packages at companies comparable to Mannesmann, did not include stock options. (There is also some indication that Fok thought giving Esser a bonus might speed up the final negotiations for the takeover.) Accordingly, Fok offered to have the Hong Kong company pay Esser a £10 million bonus. Esser rebuffed this offer, stating that, because he worked solely for Mannesmann, only Mannesmann could pay him a bonus. Esser also stated that his management team deserved to share in any bonus, and that Vodafone should approve.

Mannesmann's supervisory board had delegated the task of setting compensation for members of the management board to an executive committee of the supervisory board, called the *Prasidium*. The *Prasidium* had four members: two members who had been elected to the supervisory board by the stockholders—Josef Ackerman (a senior executive, and now CEO, at Deutsche Bank) and Joachim Funk (Esser's predecessor as CEO at Mannesmann)—and two supervisory board members selected by the Mannesmann employees—Jurgen Ladberg (chairman of the shop council for Mannesmann) and Klaus Zwickel (chairman of a labor union).

On February 4, 2000, two of the members of the *Prasidium* (Ackerman and Funk) met. Funk reported Fok's urging that Esser receive a £10 million bonus, with a similar amount to be shared among other members of Mannesmann's senior management. Funk also reported that Vodafone's management had agreed that this would be a good idea. Based upon the urging of Mannesmann's largest stockholder going into the Vodafone takeover (the Hong Kong company), and support from the company that was to buy all of Mannesmann's stock (Vodafone, to whom 21 percent of Mannesmann shares had already been tendered), Funk and Ackerman agreed to this bonus (labeled an appreciation award). Funk then called Zwickel. Zwickel thought Esser deserved something, but that the proposed £10 million bonus was too large. Nevertheless, because Zwickel felt that the bonus did not relate to employee concerns, and because he did not want to obstruct the bonus, he abstained—recognizing that his participation without a negative vote allowed the *Prasidium* to adopt the bonus.

When the German press heard about the bonus—as a result of disclosure required of Vodafone under English law—the result was widespread and largely negative commentary. As result of this negative publicity, the *Prasidium* discussed the bonus again at meetings on February 17 and 28, while Ackerman briefed the employee representatives on Mannesmann's supervisory board about the bonus at the supervisory board's meeting on February 17. Employee reaction to the bonus was negative, and, outside of the meetings, Ladberg (the member of the *Prasidium* who had not been involved with the bonus decision) told some employees that he was upset about the bonus. At the *Prasidium* meetings themselves, Zwickel sought to have his action characterized as "having taken the matter under advisement." No effort was made to rescind the bonus, however, and, after Mannesmann's outside auditors were assured that Zwickel's re-labeled action was the equivalent of an abstention, Mannesmann, on March 28, 2000, paid Esser the bonus.

On March 7, 2000, a German attorney filed a criminal complaint with the Dusseldorf federal attorney's office against Klaus Esser and others. (Interestingly, this attorney's practice focused on smaller German companies. According to observers of the German scene, there has been considerable resentment at these companies toward the generous severance packages awarded to senior executives of larger corporations.) It was not until almost three years later, however, that the federal attorney brought charges. On February 17, 2003, the federal attorney filed charges against Ackermann, Funk, Zwickel, Ladberg, Esser and Dietmar Droste (Mannesmann's chief officer for personnel). The prosecutor charged that, in approving the bonus payment, Ackermann, Funk and Zwickel had violated Section 266 of the German Penal Code. This section provides:

Breach of Trust (*Untreue*)

(1) Any person who by law, administrative delegation or contract has dispositional power over the assets of others or power to commit these assets to a third party, abuses and breaches the duty laid on him by law, administrative delegation or trust relationship to protect the property interests of another, and in this way causes damage to the property interests that he should protect, shall be punished with arrest of up to five years or with a monetary fine.

The remaining defendants were charged with aiding the breach of trust.

The case was tried in a Dusseldorf criminal trial court in the first half of 2004. The trial court issued a judgment acquitting all of the defendants. The trial court concluded that, while the directors breached their duty in awarding the bonus, nevertheless they were not criminally liable because there must be an "aggravated" breach of duty in order for a business judgment to violate Section 266 of the Penal Code. In this case, the trial court found the breach was not aggravated because the company's profits were high and the continuity and the profitability of the company were never threatened, the decision was made diligently and in a transparent manner in accordance with the allocation of responsibility within the company, and the members of the Supervisory Board did not have an unlawful purpose. The prosecution appealed the case to Germany's High Court, Criminal Division, on the basis that the trial court had incorrectly interpreted the law.

Discussion:

The court began its analysis by discussing the finding of the trial court that the defendants, Funk, Ackermann and Zwickel, by granting the bonus, violated their duty to look after the trusted assets (*Vermögensbe-treuungspflicht*) of Mannesmann AG within the meaning of Section 266.]

The members of the Executive Committee (*Prasidium*) of the Supervisory Board, which represents the Stock Corporation when dealing with the members of the management board in the course of arranging the contracts of employment with the members of the [management] board and their salary, have the duty to look after the trusted assets [of the corporation], which is a result of their position as a trustee of the stock, which is property of a third party for them. According to the Stock Corporation Act they have to act for the benefit of the company when making decisions concerning matters of salary, especially they have to preserve the interest of the company and to avoid loss. The precept, to refrain from all measures which cause a certain financial loss to the Company, is a part of—without the requirement of any further legal or contractual rules—the fiduciary duties which have to be considered mandatory by a proper and diligent member of the Executive Committee of the Supervisory Board. This duty under the Stock Corporation Act is a duty to [protect] assets belonging to a third party within the meaning of Sec. 266 para. 1 of the Penal Code.

* * *

However, resolutions of the Supervisory board on the remuneration of the members of the executive board which prove detrimental to the company do not necessarily constitute a breach of duty. Remuneration of officers is part of the executive and strategic tasks of the supervisory board and therefore generally open to a relatively wide margin of business judgment and discretion. Accepting such a margin of business judgment is called for because taking entrepreneurial decisions generally involves striking a balance between possible future risks and prospects and, due of their prospective nature, it is inherent* * *that the quality [of such decisions] sometimes can only be known in hindsight. Hence no breach of duty can be found where a decision is based on a sense of responsibility, on diligent collection of all relevant data and is aimed solely toward furthering the company's best interests. [Citing prior German cases]

* * *

As far as the approval of ex post extra payments for a task owed under the relevant employment contract, the following principles apply:

(1) If a covenant is included in the employment contract to the effect that, contingent upon economic success, a one-time or annually recurring bonus is payable as a variable component of remuneration (cf the recommendations contained in the German Corporate Governance Codex [a voluntary code of good corporate governance practices] 4.2.3.), such a bonus may be awarded retroactively for the previous year. The broad scope for business judgment is rooted in the trust relationship and

is restrained only so far as the total remuneration of a member of the management board must, in accordance with Sec. 87 AktG, be reasonably related to his tasks and to the situation of the corporation.*

(2) Even if no clause is included in the employment contract to that effect, awarding a bonus after the fact is permissible if and to the extent the company at the same time receives benefits in reasonable proportion to the reduction of corporate funds that results from the ex gratia payment. This applies in particular to additional remuneration advanced to signal to its recipient or to other active or future top management personnel that extraordinary achievements will be rewarded, that is, for the purpose of creating incentives structures that are beneficial to the corporation. Even an extra payment to a member of the management board that will soon leave the corporation may be possible as a means to create incentives for third parties. However, in such cases particular emphasis will be placed on the proportionality principle of Sec. 87 AktG. The upper limits of such compensation may not be determined in general and, given the specific facts of the current case, does not require further elaboration.

(3) A bonus payment not called for in the employment contract, as compensation for an effort owed by [the employee under] the contract [in any event], acting as a mere reward to the officer and without any prospect of future benefits to the company (payment of acknowledgment without compensation), however, must be considered squandering the company's property in breach of fiduciary duties. Such a payment is per se inadmissible without raising further questions as to whether the total remuneration received by the member of the management board, including all extra payments, is still proportionate in accordance with Sec. 87 AktG.

* * *

Based on the evidence in the ruling of the trial court, the extra payments made when the takeover had already been agreed upon; when the company was about to lose its economic independence [as a result of the takeover], and when it was clear that the current top management would be leaving the corporation, the strategy of which henceforth would be determined by Vodafone, were of no interest whatsoever to the Mannesmann Corporation. The tasks the management team had per-

---

* [Section 87 of Germany's Stock Corporation Act provides:

Principles for the Remuneration for Members of the Management Board

(1) When determining the total remuneration for each member of the Management Board (salary, participation in profits, compensation for additional efforts, insurance payments, additional payments and compensation of any kind), the Supervisory Board must ensure that the total remuneration is reasonable in relation to the tasks the member of the management board shall perform and the situation of the corporation. * * * Ed.]

formed, including the substantial improvement in the actual value of the corporation as well as additional stock market gains (which at least in part was influenced by speculative factors), had already been compensated by the remuneration agreed upon in the original employment contracts. According to these contracts, the members of the management team were obliged to make their entire work efforts available to Mannesmann Corporation. This applies equally to tasks performed in the context of a takeover battle. The extra payments could not create incentives either for the relevant members of the management team or for future top managers. In particular, the additional payment could not be used to bond these individual to the corporation. The reputation of Mannesmann Corporation in the eyes of the public was also not enhanced by the appreciation award. There was no relevant interest of all shareholders, the creditors of the corporation, the employees, or the public that could have been considered when deciding whether the members of the executive committee acted in the interest of the corporation. In particular, the additional payment was of no interest to the shareholders, because the increase in share value had already occurred independent of the appreciation award, and the exchange rate for the shares had already been determined.

Due to the fact that the payment of acknowledgment has reduced the assets of the Mannesmann AG without any compensation, the members of the Executive Committee of the Supervisory Board were not allowed to approve it. They did not have a margin of business judgment. Therefore the defendants Prof. Dr. Funk, Dr. Ackermann and Zwickel have violated their duty to look after the trusted assets according to Sec. 266 para. 1 Penal Code and thereby caused a financial loss to the company in the amount of the granted payment.

* * *

[The court then addressed the argument that the largest stockholder (Vodafone) approved of the bonus]

Due to the fact that the purpose of the actus reus of misappropriation *(Untreue)* is to save the assets which have been entrusted to a person who is not the owner, usually the duty to look after the trusted assets under Sec. 266 para. 1 Penal Code is not violated if the holder of the assets agrees to the financial loss. To be relevant within the Penal Code, the agreement to a payment of acknowledgment without compensation in the case of a Stock Corporation has to be made by the sole shareholder or the collectivity of the shareholders at the annual general meeting * * * and must not be illegal or ineffective due to other reasons.

The approval by Vodafone of the extra payments cannot eliminate Breach of Trust, because there was no approval by all shareholders or by the General Shareholder Meeting of Mannesmann Corporation. Mannesmann Corporation, whose assets the members of the Presidium were obliged to administer in trust, was, as a legal person, legally independent and owner of its own assets, which belonged to all shareholders in their entirety. According to the evidence, the General Meeting did not approve the payment. The acquirer, Vodafone Corporation, which at the time it approved the transaction in February 2000 held only 9.8 percent of all shares and at the time the payments were made at the end of March 2000 had become with 98.66 percent of shares only a controlling shareholder, became the sole shareholder of Mannesmann Corporation only in 2002 after all shareholders had been paid out. This is not sufficient for an approval that would eliminate damages to the corporation's assets, as such an approval must be given in advance. The approval of a future shareholders thus is of no relevance for whether the defendants are guilty—but it may considered in determining the level of punishment * * *.

[The court then addresses the trial court's decision to acquit based upon the lack of an "aggravated" breach.]

The opinion of the [lower] criminal court cannot be followed to the extent that it states that, in the context of business judgments involving risk, a finding of breach of trust requires the additional element of an "aggravated" breach of duty, which here must be evaluated taking into account the overall picture, particularly the healthy state of the profits and assets of Mannesmann AG, the preservation of transparency within the company, and that the members of the executive committee (*Präsidium*) were duly informed of the facts necessary for their decision, as well as the absence of impermissible motives.

* * *

Defendants Prof. Dr. Funk, Dr. Ackermann and Mr. Zwickel were not presented with a business judgment involving risk as described by the lower court when they resolved to grant appreciation awards for the Defendant Dr. Esser and the four other members of the management board. The granting of the awards had—as explained above—an exclusively negative impact on the assets of Mannesmann AG that had been given into their trust. No foreseeable advantage, even if unintended, could have been hoped for the company under the circumstances presented in this case. The executive committee thus had no room for free judgment. For a case of this type, it is certain—even in light of the [German criminal court case authority cited by the trial court to support its decision]—that a manager can violate his duty to care for entrusted assets pursuant to § 266(1) of the Criminal Code without an "aggravating" violation of duty having the slightest significance.

[In other portions of the opinion, the court dealt with Zwickel's argument that he had not voted for the bonus. The court pointed out that Zwickel knew his presence was necessary to grant the bonus, and that, although he abstained from voting for the remuneration, he had the intent to make the resolution effective simply by being present.

The High Court sent the case back to the trial court to retry the issue of the defendants' knowledge that the bonus was illegal. The defendants argued that, given the market practice of granting bonuses, they could not have known that the bonus was illegal. The legal basis for this ignorance of the law defense comes from Section 17 of the German Penal Code. This section provides: "If an actor does not know at the time she performs an act that she is violating a prohibition, she acts without guilt if her error was unavoidable. * * * "]

Notes

1. Compare the outcome of *Mannesmann* with the outcome in *In re The Walt Disney Company Derivative Litigation*, 2006 WL 1562466 (Del.). Is there something wrong with this picture: In *Disney* the Delaware court exonerated the directors of Disney, from liability for damages despite their having approved a compensation package for Michael Ovitz that resulted in Ovitz receiving around $140 million in exchange for having spent a year accomplishing little as the number two executive at Disney. By contrast, the directors of Mannesman face fines and even prison for having awarded a £10 million (approximately $17 million) bonus to Klaus Esser—despite the fact that Esser's actions as CEO apparently played an important role in increasing the price that the Mannesmann shareholders received from the Vodafone takeover by 63 billion euros (over $50 *billion*).

In considering the broader implications of the comparison between *Mannesmann* and *Disney*, it is interesting to note that in 2000, the average CEO in the United States received 531 times the pay of an average employee in his or her company, while, in Germany, the average CEO received only 11 times the pay of an average employee in his or her company. Does the difference in the outcomes in *Mannesmann* and *Disney* suggest some difference in law that might help explain this difference in pay scales, or does the difference in pay scales help one understand the difference in the outcomes despite similar law in *Mannesmann* and *Disney*; or perhaps a little of both? Is there some underlying cultural or even philosophical difference at work here: Should society focus on how much Esser received as a bonus, or how much the shareholders received as a result of the Vodafone takeover? Put differently, is equality or wealth creation the critical underlying value?

Or perhaps what is at work is nothing more than a minor technical point of law regarding which one can find analogous cases in the United States. *Compare Mannesmann, with Adams v. Smith*, 153 So.2d 221 (Ala. 1963) (finding a corporation's gratuitous award of pensions to widows after their husbands had died to be ultra vires).

2. The bonus to Esser (and, indeed, all compensation to senior executives) represents just one example of the much broader set of transactions that occur between corporations and those charged with the corporations' management. Corporate laws in different nations take a number of common approaches to protect corporations that enter into transactions with their

managers and directors—so-called conflict-of-interest transactions—albeit nations differ in how they mix and match and apply these approaches:

(i) *Categorical Condemnation*

A simple-minded approach to dealing with conflict-of-interest transactions would be to issue a blanket condemnation of all such transactions based upon a generalized suspicion that the conflicted managers are likely to favor their own interest at the expense of the corporation and it is not worth the effort to separate out the rare exception. While some older court opinions in the United States suggest such a rule, no nation actually takes this approach. *E.g.*, Luca Enriques, *The Law on Corporate Directors' Self-Dealing: A Comparative Analysis*, 2 Int'l & Comp. Corp. L. J. 297 (2000). To understand why no nation takes this approach, ask what would happen if the type of conflict-of-interest transaction involved in *Mannesmann*—executive compensation—was automatically condemned, even if what was involved was the salary in the CEO's contract.

A number of nations take a more focused approach by automatically condemning certain types of conflict-of-interest transactions. A common target are loans from a corporation to its managers. *E.g.*, Companies Act, 1985, c. 6, § 330 (Eng.); Code de commerce art. L. 223–21, 225–43 (France). Why do a number of nations single out such loans for per se condemnation? While state corporate law restrictions on such loans had long been on the wane in the United States, the recent Sarbanes–Oxley Act resurrected the prohibition in the United States, at least for public corporations.

(ii) *Disinterested Director Approval*

The facts in *Mannesmann* illustrate a second type of protection for the corporation in the case of conflict-of-interest transactions: This being approval by directors who are not in a conflict. German corporate law illustrates some potentially significant differences between the use of disinterested director approval in many countries outside of the United States, and its use in the United States.

To begin with, the German statute requires, rather then simply allows, members of the management board to obtain approval from the supervisory board in order to enter any transactions with the corporation. Aktiengesetz § 112. Even many nations whose corporate laws do not call for two-tier boards require approval by disinterested directors of transactions between the corporation and members of the board. *E.g.*, Shoho [Commercial Code], art. 265(1) (Japan); Code de commerce art. L. 225–38 (France). *But see id.* at art. L. 225–39 (exempting "current transactions entered into at normal conditions" from the requirement of disinterested director and shareholder approval in France). While laws in the United States a century ago also commonly required disinterested director approval for conflict-of-interest transactions, compare the rule generally prevailing in the United States today.

Next, notice the seemingly elegant way in which the German two-tier board appears to answer various questions that arise in the United States in applying the concept of disinterested director approval. As mentioned in the last Chapter (dealing with Corporate Governance Structures), the German two-tier board creates a separate supervisory board, none of whose members can sit on the management board (which is charged with the actual management of the company). By then delegating to the supervisory board the task of representing the corporation in any dealings with members of the management board (such as approving compensation), the German corporate statute seemingly answers automatically the questions that arise under corporate statutes in the United States as far as who is a disinterested director and how many disinterested directors must vote to approve a conflict-of-interest transaction. Yet, can things ever be this simple? Might there be some relations—financial, family, or just influence over elections—between the managing and supervisory board members that would raise questions about the disinterest of the latter?

As *Mannesmann* illustrates, disinterested director approval rarely completely insulates a conflict-of-interest transaction from any judicial review. What was the evident impact of disinterested director approval on judicial review in *Mannesmann*? What would be the impact in the United States?

(iii) *Shareholder Approval*

The court in *Mannesmann* notes that stockholder approval of the transaction could have avoided liability for the defendants, but no such approval occurred for the simple reason that the stockholders never voted on the bonus. Given the fact that Vodafone—which would ultimately own all of the outstanding Mannesmann stock, and out of whose pocket, at least indirectly, the bonus would come—approved of the bonus, was the court being too technical? In any event, putting a conflict-of-interest transaction to a shareholder vote is a third mechanism for protecting the corporation. Once again, there are potentially important differences between corporate laws found inside and outside of the United States with respect to this mode of protection.

As was the case with disinterested director approval, shareholder approval of conflict-of-interest transactions is required in some nations, rather than just optional as is the case for the most part in the United States. *E.g.*, Code de commerce art. L. 225–40 (France requires both disinterested director and shareholder approval). Another difference from corporate statutes in most of the United States arises in the willingness of corporate laws in some nations to count the shares voted by the directors who are in the conflict-of-interest. *E.g.*, Shoho [Commercial Code] art. 247(1)(iii) (Japanese law permits voting of shares owned by directors in a conflict, but the court may nullify the transaction if interested voting results in a "significantly unfair" outcome). Is this Japanese law different from the Delaware Supreme Court's approach in *Fliegler v. Lawrence*, 361 A.2d 218 (Del. 1976) (shares voted by directors in a conflict-of-interest count for purposes of meeting the Delaware statute validating conflict-of-interest transactions, but the court nevertheless will review the fairness of a conflict-of-interest transaction that received shareholder approval only by virtue of the votes cast by the interested directors)? Finally, consider the suggestion in *Mannesmann* that a shareholder vote could have insulated the directors from liability for what the court found to be, in effect, giving away corporate assets for no business purpose. Is this consistent with law in the United States—at least for anything less than a unanimous vote?

(iv) *Judicial Review of the Merits of the Transaction*

The court's condemnation of the bonus in *Mannesmann* on the ground that the corporation got nothing in exchange for its money is an example of a fourth protection that the law can afford to corporations in the case of conflict-of-interest transactions: This being a review by a court (or some other agency of government) of the merits of the transaction from the standpoint of the corporation. A key issue in such a review is what standard the court will apply. In *Mannesmann*, the court concluded that the lack of any benefit meant that the decision flunked even the margin allowed to the directors' business judgment. Keeping in mind the composition of the committee that approved the bonus to Esser, would a court have applied the business judgment rule to this transaction in the United States?

In the United States, the quid pro quo for upholding a conflict-of-interest transaction in the absence of disinterested director or shareholder approval is judicial review of the conflict-of-interest transaction under a highly intrusive fairness test, in which the conflicted directors must convince a skeptical court of the merits of the transaction. The corollary to the laws in many other nations that require, rather than simply allow, disinterested director or shareholder approval of conflict-of-interest transactions is that there is less occasion for courts outside the United States to undertake such an intrusive fairness review. Are there some reasons why other nations may place somewhat more emphasis on disinterested director or shareholder approval, while the corporate laws in the United States may place somewhat greater reliance on judicial review, as mechanisms to protect corporations that enter conflict-of-interest transactions? Could this reflect broader systemic differences in the willingness of common law and civil law legal regimes to rely on judicial development and application of variable standards?

(v) *After-the-fact Disclosure*

One last mechanism often claimed to protect corporations from bad deals in conflict-of-interest transactions is the requirement in some corporate or securities laws that those in charge of the company disclose to shareholders, or to financial markets generally, such transactions. For example, both in the United States and the European Union, regulators recently have put forward proposals to increase corporate reporting of executive compensation. *E.g.*, http://www.europa.eu.int/comm/internal_market/company/directors-remun/index_en.htm (European Commission proposal for European Union listed companies to disclose executive pay policy and individual director compensation). How can such an after-the-fact disclosure serve to limit bad deals in conflict-of-interest transactions? Looking at the experience of professional athletes, might widespread publication of compensation actually increase, rather than decrease, the amount corporations pay?

3. Compare the application of a business judgment rule in *Mannesmann*, as well as *Garmenbeck*, with the application of the rule in typical cases in the United States. Do the German courts show a greater willingness to dissect the directors' decisions and compare them against the courts' own logic template then one might expect from courts applying the business judgment rule in the United States?

4. Finally, compare the remedy sought in *Mannesmann* with that sought in *Disney*. What is the rationale for criminal sanctions, especially

against those who did not profit from the bonus? Are there some practical advantages, both in terms of who decides to bring the action, and in terms of the consequences, for a criminal prosecution over a derivative suit? Are there some practical disadvantages?

SECTION B. TRANSACTIONS WITH CONTROL-LING SHAREHOLDERS

JOHN LYONS, MEXICO MOVES TO TIGHTEN LAWS OVER SECURITIES

Wall Street Journal A14 (December 8, 2005).*

MEXICO CITY—Mexico's lower house of Congress approved a sweeping overhaul of the nation's securities laws designed to strengthen oversight by corporate boards, increase transparency and stiffen regulatory enforcement in a country whose clubby business practices long have been criticized as rigged to favor large shareholders.

* * *

Since tying itself to the U.S. economy through the North American Free Trade Agreement in 1994, Mexico has sought to portray itself as a trustworthy market for international investment. But unlike their counterparts in the U.S. and elsewhere, most big Mexican firms are still family-run, creating a business culture where the controlling family's interests often trump those of smaller investors. Laws have provided few protections against shareholder abuse.

* * *

In a World Bank ranking of minority-shareholder protections this year, Mexico ranked 125th out of 155 countries—worse than Haiti. The new law would boost Mexico's ranking about 85 notches, to 40th in the world, according to a recent World Bank review of the bill solicited by Mexican officials.

It remains to be seen how effectively Mexican regulators would use their new powers. White-collar crimes seldom are prosecuted in Mexico. Federal authorities have never even sought a criminal conviction for insider trading, for instance, even though the practice became a crime in 2001.

After Washington enacted Sarbanes–Oxley in 2002, Mexican officials started pushing for a similar version. Officials here believe the country's reputation for rigged markets long has scared away foreign investors. Investment in Mexico's stock market has been so anemic in recent years that more companies have delisted than issued new shares. Overall, foreign direct investment in Mexico is at its lowest annual level since the mid–1990s and the country attracts only 10% of the venture capital going to Latin America.

Opposition to the proposed law was led by [billionaire media executive Ricardo] Salinas [Pliego], the 50–year-old chairman of Mexico's second biggest broadcaster, TV Azteca SA. Mr. Salinas is the first executive of a foreign company sued by U.S. officials for violating the Sarbanes–Oxley law. The fraud allegations in a civil lawsuit filed by the U.S. Securities and Exchange Commission relate to a 2003 deal whereby Mr. Salinas used a shell company to buy debt for pennies on the dollar from a cellphone company he controlled, Unefon SA. He then sold the debt back to Unefon at full price a few months later, pocketing $109 million profit at expense of other shareholders. U.S. officials got involved because one of Unefon's main shareholders was TV Azteca, which traded at the time on the New York Stock Exchange.

The transaction was largely legal in Mexico under existing laws. The new law, however, would have forced Mr. Salinas to disclose his involvement in the shell company to outside directors. [The bill, among other things, requires publicly traded companies to set up committees of independent board members to review executive compensation and related-party transactions.]

* * *

Note

A curiosity in this news story is what the United States' Sarbanes–Oxley Act has to do with Mexican legislation, a central feature of which is to require independent director review of conflict-of-interest transactions. In fact, the Sarbanes–Oxley Act—whose focus is on improving the accuracy of information disclosed to investors by listed corporations, including by requiring independent directors to be on corporate board audit committees that select and deal with outside accountants—contains no provision requiring independent director review of conflict-of-interest transactions. (Hence, the prosecution of Mr. Salinas under the Sarbanes–Oxley Act is not based upon his having profited at Unefon's and TV Azteca's expense, but, rather, is based upon his failing to disclose fully the transaction to investors. S.E.C. Release No. 19022, 2005 WL 20420.) Were the Mexican officials, who purportedly were pushing for a law similar to the Sarbanes–Oxley Act, unaware of what the Sarbanes–Oxley Act contained; or is this like one of those movies supposedly "inspired by a true story"?

This, in turn, leads one to ask why the Mexican legislation focused more on transactions with related parties, while the United States legislation focused more on the accuracy of corporate disclosure to investors. In the United States, in which stock options have come to dominate the compensation of senior executives, what temptation results with respect to reporting financial results that can impact the price of the corporation's shares on the stock market? By contrast, according to the news story, how did Mr. Salinas purportedly utilize his control over the company to profit? Indeed, some empirical scholarly work has suggested that controlling shareholders in Mexico expropriate approximately half the value of Mexican companies. *E.g.*, Ronald J. Gilson, *Controlling Shareholders and Corporate Governance: Complicating the Comparative Taxonomy* 9 (August 2005), ECGI—Law Working

Paper No. 49/2005, available at SSRN: http://ssrn.com/abstract=784744. Is such expropriation through transactions between corporations and their controlling shareholders confined to Mexico? To corporations in the developing world? Have laws in developed countries better dealt with such expropriation?

JOHNSON, LA PORTA, LOPEZ–DE–SILANES & SHLEIFER, TUNNELING

90 Am. Econ. Rev. 22 (2000).

* * * In this paper, we use the term "tunneling," coined originally to characterize the expropriation of minority shareholders in the Czech Republic (as in removing assets through an underground tunnel), to describe the transfer of assets and profits out of firms for the benefit of those who control them.

* * *

II.　Cases on Tunneling

In this section, we will discuss several well-known cases of tunneling in Western European countries, which are generally taken by legal scholars as indicative of how the courts see the law.

1. *SARL Peronnet* (Corporate Opportunities).—SAICO, a minority shareholder of SARL Peronnet, a French company controlled by the Peronnet family, sued the directors from the Peronnet family. The Peronnet family established a new company, SCI, solely owned by family members. SCI bought some land and took out a loan to build a warehouse. SCI then leased the warehouse to SARL Peronnet, which expanded its business and used the proceeds to repay the loan. The plaintiff argued that the Peronnet family expropriated the corporate opportunity of SARL Peronnet (namely, to build a warehouse) and thereby benefited itself at the expense of minority shareholders.

The court ruled against SAICO, on two grounds. First, it held that the decision by Peronnet to pay SCI to warehouse its products was not against the social interest, as evidenced by the fact that sales of SARL Peronnet expanded during this period. Second, the court held that SARL Peronnet's expansion had benefited SAICO as well. It could thus be argued that the decision to build a warehouse through SCI was not taken with the sole intention of benefiting the majority shareholders (i.e., the Peronnet family) and had a legitimate business purpose. Under French law, this was sufficient to rule against SAICO. The court took no interest in the questions of whether the creation of SCI, and the prices it charged SARL Peronnet for the use of the warehouse, were fair to SAICO and other minority shareholders. The court took a very particular interpretation of the effect of the deal on the minority shareholders of SARL Peronnet: as long as they have not suffered an actual loss, the business judgment rule protected the Peronnet family. In the United States and the United Kingdom, courts would be very suspicious of the conduct of the Peronnet family unless it could demonstrate that it closely mimicked an arms-length transaction through an independent valuation of the lease or approval by independent directors.

2. *Marcilli* (Transfer Pricing).—Marcelli, an Italian machinery maker, was 51–percent owned by its controlling shareholder, Sarcem, a Swiss machinery maker, and 49–percent owned by two minority shareholders, Luigi Anguissola and Alberto Mignani (the plaintiffs), who sat on the board. Philip Bonello, the President and CEO of Sarcem, also became President of Marcilli in 1982. Shortly afterward, the plaintiffs resigned from the board, and sued Sarcem. They demanded a court inspection and intervention, since the absence of derivative suits made it impossible for minority shareholders to seek damages without the consent of Sarcem. The plaintiffs alleged that Sarcem, among other things: (i) precluded Marcilli from exporting its products directly, requiring that they only be sold through Sarcem; (ii) charged too high a markup for Marcilli products it resold, compromising Marcilli's market share and pocketing short-term profits; (iii) sold and exhibited Marcilli products under its own trademark; (iv) overcharged Marcilli for the services it provided such as costs of participating in international fairs; and (v) did not pay Marcilli for its goods on time.

The court declined to appoint a judicial investigator since it found that the influence exerted by the majority shareholder was consistent with a group policy, and therefore a well-defined and explicit business discipline could not be excluded. In deciding for Sarcem, the court focused on the duty of care, with two further twists favoring the defendant. First, the duty of Marcilli's President (Bonello) was to the group including Sarcem rather than to the shareholders of Marcilli. Second, since the issues involved day-to-day business transactions as opposed to explicit board decisions, none of the statutory rules governing conflicts of interest kicked in, because these rules only apply to resolutions of collective organs (shareholders' meetings or boards of directors). Again, no fairness test was used, and the court sanctioned tunneling from a company to its controlling shareholder through transfer pricing.

3. *Flambo and Barro* (The Plunder of Barro).—A French firm, Flambo, was the controlling shareholder in a Belgian company, Barro. Several significant minority shareholders of Barro (the plaintiffs) sued Flambo, arguing that it literally stripped Barro of its assets, and demanded judicial intervention and remedies. The plaintiffs argued that Flambo: (i) tried to pledge Barro (i.e., the whole company) as collateral to guarantee Flambo's debt; (ii) forced Barro to acquire all of the new shares of Flambo in a capital increase; (iii) withdrew a substantial sum from Barro's accounts without subsequent repayment; (iv) diverted an important contract with Rank Xerox from Barro to Flambo; and (v) made use of the utilities belonging to Barro without paying for them.

Since Belgium has no statutory rules relating to intergroup transactions, the court relied on the business judgment rule and held that Flambo's conduct was consistent with the interest of the group as a whole. The court pointed out that, in principle, it was not objectionable for a subsidiary to support its parent as long as the subsidiary itself was not in danger of bankruptcy. Fairness to the minority shareholders of Barro did not come up in the ruling, and while the court disallowed Flambo to continue transferring resources from Barro without judicial review, it did not propose any remedies for past expropriation or even a change in Barro's board. As in the previous case, the court took a broad view of the interests of the group rather than the subsidiary company and therefore (up to a limit) saw no problem with the tunneling of resources out of a subsidiary to the controlling shareholder.

[4. *Audi* (Transactions in Stock)] * * * In another famous case, Volkswagen, the controlling (75–percent) shareholder of Audi, bought out a small equity stake of a minority shareholder in Audi for 145 DM per share. The price was based on a valuation provided by Volkswagen. Two weeks later, Volkswagen bought out a very large (14–percent) stake in Audi from the British–Israeli Bank for 220 DM per share. The German Supreme Court refused to hear the complaint from the small shareholder on the grounds that the controlling shareholder did not owe any duties of good faith or loyalty to the minority shareholders. The court also agreed that Volkswagen was under no obligation to reveal its negotiations with the British–Israeli Bank, because such a revelation might have negatively affected the valuation of Volkswagen's shares.

* * *

Notes

1. The authors of this article are not lawyers. Are they correct that these four examples suggest a greater willingness of courts in some European nations to sanction "tunneling" than would courts in the United States?

Start with the *SARL Peronnet* decision. Is it clear that a court in the United States would have found the opportunity to build a warehouse belonged to the corporation that would lease the warehouse after its construction? Are the authors of the article on more solid ground when they state that a court in the United States would have demanded the defendants prove, at least in the absence of independent director approval, that the lease price they charged the corporation they controlled equaled an arms length deal? See *Lewis v. S.L. & E., Inc.*, 629 F.2d 764 (2d Cir. 1980) (the court held that controlling shareholders of a corporation, which leased its property to another corporation they owned, breached their duty when they failed to prove that the rent was fair as measured by rents in arms-length transactions). *But see Cookies Food Products, Inc. v. Lakes Warehouse Distributing, Inc.*, 430 N.W.2d 447 (Iowa 1988) (the court found transactions between the corporation and a company owned by the corporation's majority shareholder to be fair, despite the fact that the corporation could have obtained many of the services provided by the majority shareholder's company cheaper, when the overall effort by the majority shareholder's company to distribute the corporation's product had been instrumental in turning a struggling operation into a successful one).

Similarly, what standard would a court in the United States have used to evaluate the various transactions involved in the *Marcilli* and *Barro* decisions? Would a court in the United States have applied the business judgment rule, or demanded that the defendants prove the fairness of these transactions? Would the court have allowed benefit to the parent to weigh against cost to the subsidiary? See *Sinclair Oil Corp. v. Levien*, 280 A.2d 717 (Del. 1971) (transactions in which the parent corporation gains something to the exclusion of the minority shareholders constitute self-dealing and call for application of the intrinsic fairness test; parent flunked this test when it could not prove that the *subsidiary's* interest mandated the subsidiary's failure to enforce, *to the letter*, a requirements contract made with an affiliated corporation). Incidently, compare the *Marcilli, Barro* and *Sinclair* decisions with the Canadian Supreme Court's decision in *Peoples Department Stores*, reprinted earlier in this Chapter. Did the Canadian Supreme Court review whether the transactions between the Wise and Peoples department store companies—particularly insofar as Peoples ended up effectively extending significant trade credit to Wise—matched an arms length deal?

Finally, compare the *Audi* decision with *Rochez Bros., Inc. v. Rhoades*, 491 F.2d 402 (3d Cir. 1973) (50% shareholder, who bought out the other 50% shareholder, violated Rule 10B–5 by failing to disclose negotiations with a third party to sell the corporation at a higher price).

2. In the discussion of executive compensation earlier in this Chapter, did it seem that corporate laws outside the United States were more lax than corporate laws inside the United States in dealing with conflicts-of-interest? If not, what explains these tunneling cases?

Recall that corporate laws outside of the United States often place critical reliance on disinterested director and shareholder approval as tools to protect the corporation when the company enters into a contract with a director; in contrast to the corporate laws inside the United States, in which courts have developed a tradition of strict judicial review of the fairness of the transaction as at least a co-equal avenue of protection. Is there any reason to think that either approach necessarily provides significantly greater protection when the conflict-of-interest involves simply one or more directors entering a contract with the corporation? Now, however, consider what changes if the transaction involves a controlling shareholder—who has elected (and can remove) the entire board, and who has enough votes to pass a resolution approving the transaction. In this instance, is reliance on disinterested director and shareholder approval sufficient? Might courts that have not developed a tradition of applying strict fairness review in the context of director conflicts have some difficulty switching to such an approach when the transaction involves a controlling shareholder?

Alternately, perhaps the explanation is that we need to be more refined in differentiating between various nations outside of the United States. Notice that the *SARL Peronnet, Marcilli* and *Barro* decisions involve the corporate laws of France, Italy and Belgium, respectively. Notice also that one significant dilution of the protection accorded to the subsidiary by the *Marcilli* and *Barro* decisions comes from the view of the courts in those cases that the subsidiaries' directors can sacrifice the subsidiaries' interest (within limits) for the good of the overall groups of companies (including the parents). In fact, even though apparently not applied by the French court in the *SARL Peronnet* decision, the view that directors of a subsidiary can sacrifice, within limits, the subsidiary's interest for the good of the group is often referred to as the *Rozenblum* doctrine, from the name of the case in which the French Supreme Court announced this rule. Specifically, in a criminal case brought against directors of a French corporation for *"abus de biens sociaux"* (abuse of trust), the French Supreme Court stated that siphoning assets between related corporations would not be an abuse of trust if supported by an "economic social or financial common interest" of "the group as a whole;" so long as the siphoning was not "devoid of any return" and did not "disrupt the balance of mutual obligations of the companies involved," "nor exceed the financial capacity of the company" from which the assets came. Cass (fr) 4 February 1985 [1985] Dalloz 478, translated in Eddy Wymeersch, *Do We Need a Law on Groups of Companies?* in CAPITAL MARKETS AND COMPANY LAW 590–91 (2003).

By contrast, the German law of corporate groups (Konzern) seems more protective. Chapter III discussed the German law regarding Konzern with respect to its impact on the limited liability of parent corporations and the protection of creditors of subsidiary companies. This law also acts to protect minority shareholders in subsidiaries. For example, a German firm, which controls a German marketable stock company (an AG), must compensate the subsidiary AG for any losses incurred by the subsidiary in any transactions the parent causes the subsidiary to undertake—unless (in a rule that should sound familiar) a prudent manager of an independent company would have made the same deal. Aktiengesetz §§ 311, 317. (This situation is referred to as a defacto Konzern.) To help enforce this obligation, the statute requires the subsidiary's management board to prepare an annual report analyzing all transactions with, or at the behest of, the parent or other affiliated companies during the year. *Id.* at § 312. Parent corporations can avoid these provisions by entering a domination agreement with the subsidiary, under which the parent can manage the subsidiary without regard to the subsidiary's interest. (This is the so-called contractual Konzern.) The quid pro quo, however, for such an agreement is that the parent must cover any losses the subsidiary suffers every year, and the minority stockholders have the right to demand the parent cash them out. *Id.* at §§ 302, 305, 308.

3.   From a legal or policy standpoint, should it matter whether tunneling by controlling shareholders reflects simple greed, versus the desire of a family to preserve a business empire by having stronger companies under family control bail out weaker ones? Notice how the *Rozenblum* doctrine might draw this distinction. Such family motivations seem to have played an important role in recent corporate meltdowns in places like Indonesia. *E.g.,* Benny S. Tabalujan, *Why Indonesian Corporate Governance Failed—Conjectures Concerning Legal Culture*, 15 Colum. J. Asian L. 141 (2002). Suppose the controlling shareholder is the government—as in semi-privatized corporations in China. Should social or political motivations for channeling corporate assets into activities desired by the government be beyond review? Is there some economic inefficiency created when economic actors do not at least attempt to treat each transaction with other economic actors as if made with a stranger? Can families or governments expect strangers to invest in corporations run too much for family or governmental motivations?

SECTION C. ENFORCEMENT OF CLAIMS AGAINST DIRECTORS AND CONTROLLING SHAREHOLDERS

ARAG/GARMENBECK CASE

BGHZ 135, 244 (Bundesgerichtshof [Federal Court of Justice], F.R.G. 1997).
Translated in Andreas Cahn & David C. Donald, COMPARATIVE COMPANY LAW
(forthcoming).

[The facts of this case can be found at pages 80–81 *supra.*]

DISCUSSION:

* * *

1.   * * *

[T]he Court of Appeals found that a supervisory board member had a legal right to seek a declaratory judgment on the nullity of a supervisory board resolution because of its contents only if the rights of such supervisory board *qua* member were violated or limited, or if the supervisory board refused to comply with a shareholders' resolution adopted pursuant to § 147(1) AktG to take recourse against a member of the management board. Since the facts here do not present a like situation, the Court of Appeals found that the Plaintiffs did not have standing to seek a declaratory judgment. We disagree with that holding.

a) We need not address at this time whether a supervisory board member may obtain standing on the basis of his personal interest to distance himself from a supervisory board resolution so as to avoid being sued in possible challenges under § 116 AktG for aiding and abetting the illegal actions of a management body. * * * In any case, the interest of a supervisory board member to seek such a judgment flows from his or her position on the board and the related common responsibility for the legality of the resolutions that body adopts. A supervisory board member has not only the right and duty to fulfill his assigned tasks as a board member in compliance with law and the articles of association, but rather his board position also gives him at least the right to act so that the board to which he belongs makes its decisions in a way that does not violate the law or the articles of association. If a board member cannot achieve this through discussions and decision-making in the board, he then has the right to seek clarity through judicial action. The Civil Division has already made this point in an earlier decision.

* * *

c) Contrary to the holding of the Court of Appeals, standing to seek judicial remedy may not in cases like that before us be restricted to situations where the majority of the supervisory board has refused to carry out a shareholders' resolution adopted pursuant to § 147(1) AktG to exercise a claim for damages against a member of the management board. The function of the supervisory board to monitor the entire management activity of the management board—including measures already taken—creates a duty to examine existing damages claims against the management board and to act on them if they have merit (§ 111(1) AktG), as well as to represent the corporation in and out of court vis-à-vis the management board pursuant to § 112 AktG. The supervisory board is not released from this duty of examination and prosecution by the mere possibility that the shareholders' meeting may reach a decision pursuant to § 147(1) AktG with regard to exercising a damages claim against a management board member as long as the shareholders' meeting has neither exercised such right with a resolution to prosecute or waived its right to prosecute in a binding manner (§ 93(4), sentence 3, AktG). As a consequence, the right of each member of the supervisory board to submit the decision of the supervisory board for judicial examination of its legality is not prejudiced by the possibility that the shareholders' meeting could adopt a resolution pursuant to § 147(1) AktG.

* * *

Notes

1. The cases reprinted or discussed in this Chapter illustrate a wide variety of possible legal proceedings through which to address mismanagement by directors or controlling shareholders. These include: shareholder derivative suits (the *Daiwa*, *Nomura*, and *Hazama* cases from Japan); an action by a governmental official to disqualify individuals from serving as directors (the *Barings* case from England); an action by the trustee for a corporation in bankruptcy (the *Peoples Department Stores* case from Canada; in which the court also mentions the availability of a suit by creditors to remedy oppression by those in charge of the corporation); a criminal prosecution for abuse of trust (the *Mannesmann* case from Germany); a shareholder demand for a judicially ordered inspection of corporate affairs (the *Marcilli* case from Italy); and the action by the dissenting directors in the *Garmenbeck* case above to declare invalid the refusal of the board to sue the CEO (in which the court also mentions the ability of shareholders to vote to have such a suit). As this list suggests, the procedural aspects of dealing with corporate mismanagement are among the most complex and challenging facets of corporate law worldwide.

2. One fact that accounts for much of the procedural complexity of dealing with corporate mismanagement is that the logical plaintiff, the corporation, cannot speak for itself in deciding whether to bring an action against those who were, and may still be, in charge of the company. Different nations have reached different answers to the question of what to do about seeking recovery for the corporation from those accused of mismanaging the company.

A principal answer to this problem in the United States is the ability of a single shareholder to bring a derivative suit seeking recovery for the corporation. The availability of the derivative suit in the *Daiwa*, *Nomura*, and *Hazama* cases in Japan is the result of a post-World War II legal transplant; albeit, the use of such suits received a significant boost when an amendment to the Japanese Commercial Code in 1993 reduced the filing fee for derivative suits. *E.g.*, Curtis J. Milhaupt & Mark D. West, ECONOMIC ORGANIZATIONS AND CORPORATE GOVERNANCE IN JAPAN: THE IMPACT OF FORMAL AND INFORMAL RULES 9 (2004). Has the derivative suit been such an unqualified success in the United States to commend its adoption by other nations? In this regard, consider why the derivative suit in the United States is subject to a variety of special burdens not found in civil litigation generally.

The lesser reliance on the derivative suit by other common law countries owes much to the English decision in the case of *Foss v. Harbottle*, [1843] 67 Eng. Rep. 189 (Ch. D.), which held that the directors, not individual shareholders, have the authority to decide whether a company should sue. The principal exception to the rule in *Foss* is when the challenged conduct constitutes a "fraud on the minority." This entails both that the defendants' conduct involves some sort of duty of loyalty violation or abuse of power, rather than simply lack of care, and that the defendants own or otherwise can influence the votes of enough shares to prevent the stockholders from taking corrective action. *E.g.*, Bernard Black & Brain Cheffins, *Outside Director Liability Across Countries*, 14–15 (December 2004), Stanford Law and Economics Olin Working Paper No. 266, available at SSRN: http://ssrn.com/abstract=438321.

The German statutory provisions addressed in *Garmenbeck* illustrate some possible alternatives to derivative suits. Section 112 of the German Stock Company Law expressly empowers the supervisory board to represent the corporation in bringing legal actions against members of the management board. (As discussed in the prior Chapter dealing with Corporate Governance Structures, a German marketable stock company (an AG) must have both a management board to manage the company, and a supervisory board, with entirely different members, to supervise the management board.) The theory is that separation between the two boards will make members of the supervisory board willing to enforce the corporation's rights against members of the management board. The German saying "one crow does not gouge out the other crow's eye," however, may better capture the reality. *E.g.*, Theodor Baums & Kenneth E. Scott, *Taking Shareholder Protection Seriously? Corporate Governance in the United States and Germany*, 53 Am. J. Comp. L. 31, 52 (2005). Hence, *Garmenbeck* is an unusual case in the presence of supervisory board members, who not only voted to sue, but then took the matter to court when they lost the vote. If directors on a supervisory board can rarely bring themselves to enforce corporate claims against directors on an entirely separate board of managers, what does this say about the prospects for members of a unitary board, as in the United States, enforcing claims against other board members, even if the board delegates the decision to a special litigation committee?

Garmenbeck's call for court review of a supervisory board's vote not to sue creates an interesting judicial graft upon the statutory power of the supervisory board to sue members of the management board; albeit the court does not explain the mechanics of who actually would bring and control a suit in the event the trial court declared the refusal to sue was invalid. In any event, reexamine the portion of the *Garmenbeck* decision reprinted earlier in this Chapter, in which the court sets out the approach German courts must follow in assessing the validity of a supervisory board's decision not to sue members of the management board. How does the German approach compare with court decisions in the United States applying the demand rule and dealing with special litigation committees, such as *Aronson v. Lewis*, 473 A.2d 805 (Del. 1984) (in order to excuse demand, the plaintiff must plead with particularity facts that raise a reason to doubt that the directors are disinterested and independent or that their decision otherwise comes within the business judgment rule), and *Zapata Corp. v. Maldonado*, 430 A.2d 779 (Del. 1981) (in deciding whether to grant a motion to dismiss by a special litigation committee, the court will determine if the committee is independent and acting in good faith, and may then apply the court's own judgment to determine if the suit is in the best interest of the corporation)?

The court in *Garmenbeck* mentions a stockholder resolution under Section 147 of the German Stock Company Law. This provision allows a vote of the stockholders of an AG at the stockholders meeting to command a suit by the corporation against members of either board. (Incidentally, the stockholders of ARAG had voted to command such a suit, but the defendant management board members challenged the validity this vote in another proceeding.) Compare what it would take in the United States for a majority of shareholders to have the corporation sue directors. Should shareholders need to remove directors before being able to have the corporation sue directors? Why would shareholders want to retain directors whom the corporation should sue? Since commanding the directors to have the corporation sue themselves leads to obvious problems, Section 147 also empowers the stockholders to appoint, or request the court to appoint, a special representative to pursue the claim. Are there any advantages to having a judicially appointed representative, as opposed to one or more individual shareholder(s), in charge of litigation on behalf of the corporation?

At the time of the *Garmenbeck* decision, Section 147 empowered stockholders to command a suit either by a majority vote, or, interestingly enough, by a vote of ten percent of the outstanding shares (so long as the owners of the ten percent held their stock at least three months). Compare this idea that the holder(s) of a minority of the shares should be able to have the corporation sue its directors—so long as the minority owns some sizeable fraction of the corporation's outstanding stock—with the derivative suit in the United States. What are the advantages and disadvantages of requiring a minimum level of shareholding in order to force a suit against directors? What would it take to organize support from ten percent of the shareholders in a widely held corporation in the United States? (Incidentally, while corporate laws in the United States do not require a minimum level of shareholding in order to bring a derivative suit, some state laws have imposed a requirement to post security for the corporation's expenses upon derivative suit plaintiffs who own less than a specified fraction of the corporation's outstanding stock.)

In a sign of some convergence among corporate laws, a growing number of nations have allowed shareholders owning a minimum fraction of the corporation's outstanding stock—with newer statutes decreasing this minimum—to bring actions on behalf of the corporation against its directors. *E.g.*, Aktiengesetz § 148 (under a recent amendment, stockholders with one percent or 100,000 euros worth of the outstanding stock can bring a lawsuit on the corporation's behalf if evidence justifies the suspicion of illegal activities or a serious violation of the law or articles; albeit, the shareholders must first make a demand upon the board, and the board can have the suit dismissed if the board can show the court that not suing would be in the overriding interest of the company); Marco Ventoruzzo, *Experiments in Comparative Corporate Law: The Recent Italian Reform and the Dubious Virtues of a Market for Rules in the Absence of Effective Regulatory Competition*, 40 Tex. Int'l L. J. 113, 140–141 (2004) (in 1998, Italy changed its law to allow derivative suits by shareholders with at least 5% of the corporation's outstanding stock); Klaus J. Hopt, *Shareholder Rights and Remedies: A View from Germany and the Continent*, 2 Co. Fin. & Insolvency L. Rev. 261, 273 (1997) (France allowed derivative suits as early as 1966 by holders of at least five percent of the stock, while derivative suits later became available to holders of at least one percent or 50 million Belgian francs worth of stock in Belgium).

An alternative to allowing a shareholder to sue derivatively on behalf of the corporation is to allow a shareholder to demand an investigation into corporate affairs, which, if wrongdoing is found, can then lead to some remedy. This was the action sought in the *Marcilli* case discussed in the article on "tunneling" excerpted earlier in this Chapter. Under Italian law, a shareholder can obtain a judicial inspection of corporate affairs, and, if serious irregularities are found, the court will remove the directors. Codice civile art. 2409. The ability of shareholders to demand a court appointed auditor or inspector is widespread in Europe—going back to 1897 in German law. *E.g.*, Aktiengesetz § 142(2) (holders of at least 10% or 1 million euros worth of the outstanding stock can demand a court appointed auditor if there exist facts giving reason to suspect serious violations of law or the articles); Hopt, *supra* (holders of at least 10% of the outstanding stock can request an expert inspection, known as an *expert de gestion*, in France). What are the advantages and disadvantages of this procedure vis-a-vis a derivative suit as a means to deal with mismanagement? Who investigates the underlying facts, and through what procedure, in a derivative suit in the United States? Would an inspection by a court appointed expert be more or less burdensome? More of less likely to ferret out wrongdoing?

Finally, as illustrated by the *Peoples Department Stores* case reprinted earlier in this Chapter, a bankruptcy trustee can assert actions on behalf of the corporation—albeit for the ultimate benefit of the corporation's creditors—against the corporation's directors. Of course, the corporation must go bankrupt before this procedure comes into play.

3. To the extent that alleged mismanagement impacts various stakeholders in the corporation—the shareholders, creditors, even employees—then such stakeholders might seek to bring an action in their own right.

The *Peoples Department Stores* case reprinted earlier in this Chapter mentioned the Canadian corporate statute creating a judicial remedy for oppression. While the court focused on creditor remedies, this statute empowers any "security holder" (in other words, stockholder) to file a lawsuit seeking a judicial remedy for conduct "that is oppressive or unfairly prejudicial to or that unfairly disregards the interests of any security holder.... " The right of a stockholder to seek a remedy in the case of oppression should ring a familiar chord—as many corporate statutes in the United States authorize courts to dissolve corporations, order a buy-out of a complaining stockholder's interest, or order other relief, in the event of oppression by those in charge of the corporation. The right of a stockholder to seek relief from conduct that is unfairly prejudicial or that unfairly disregards a stockholder's interests also appears in Section 459 of the English Companies Act, with the result that stockholders in England sometimes employ Section 459 to avoid the strictures that *Foss* places on derivative suits. *See, e.g., Re Saul D. Harrison & Sons plc*, [1994] B.C.C. 475; [1995] 1 B.C.L.C. 14 (CA (Civ. Div.)) (involving a lawsuit based upon allegations that directors kept a failing corporation going, rather than winding up, so as to maintain their salaries and perquisites).

Such actions are often available to shareholders in private companies in civil law nations as well. For example, the French statute governing private companies provides for corporate dissolution for "valid reasons," such as non-performance of a member's obligation or discord paralyzing operation of the company; while the German statute governing the GmbH similarly provides for dissolution for important reasons (*wichtige Grund*). Fearing dissolution as a draconian remedy, German courts—in an approach similar to a number of cases in the United States—have ordered lesser remedies of buy-out or expulsion of shareholders in lieu of dissolution. Application of these remedies, however, often is as much or more about resolving differences among shareholders as it is addressing mismanagement. For example, even putting aside application of the expulsion remedy against a Jewish shareholder in an infamous 1942 case, German courts have found important reasons for expulsion on grounds that seem to have little to do with corporate mismanagement—including, in one case, the defendant's adultery. *E.g.*, Sandra K. Miller, *Minority Shareholder Oppression in the Private Company in the European Community: A Comparative Analysis of the German, United Kingdom, and French "Close Corporation Problem"*, 30 Cornell Int'l L.J. 381, 396–400, 408–09 (1997).

Moving beyond shareholders, the Canadian Supreme Court's suggestion in *Peoples Department Stores* that the directors owe creditors a duty of care could carry the implication that creditors have standing to sue directors without relying on the bankruptcy trustee to pursue the claim—and, indeed, even before the corporation is bankrupt. Even if that is not what the court meant, the Canadian Supreme Court's statement that creditors can invoke the statutory oppression claim yields this result. In fact, nations other than Canada have recognized the right of creditors to bring an action against directors—which, in a few nations, might allow creditor claims against directors without waiting for bankruptcy. *E.g.*, Aktiengesetz § 93(5) (allowing unpaid creditors of German marketable stock companies to sue directors); Shoho [Commercial Code], art. 266–3 (similar for Japan).

Finally, as mentioned earlier in this Chapter, the Netherlands has provided the broadest stakeholder right to redress by empowering works councils to challenge, in a special Amsterdam court, actions by Dutch corporations that are contrary to the employees' interest.

To what extent are such separate actions an appropriate response to mismanagement? If directors are asleep at the switch, make a grossly negligent business decision, or enrich themselves at the expense of the corporation, is there some problem with separate suits by shareholders, creditors and employees, each claiming some individual harm?

4. To what extent can shareholders waive, rather than pursue, claims of mismanagement? *Garmenbeck* mentions the ability of shareholders to waive claims against the directors. In fact, however, German law significantly limits the ability of shareholders to grant such a waiver: It can only occur for claims more than three years old, and only if holders of ten percent of the stock do not object. Aktiengesetz § 93(4).

Compare corporate law in much of the United States. In reaction to the imposition of liability on directors in the *Van Gorkom* decision, the Delaware legislature added Section 102(b)(7) to the Delaware General Corporation Law. As a result of this action—which many other states copied—shareholders are able to limit the liability of directors for breaching their duty of care through a provision in the corporate charter. Is there any reason to prefer the German limitations on the ability of a majority of shareholders to waive corporate claims against directors?

Recall that the *Daiwa* decision in Japan, discussed earlier in this Chapter, led to a judgment against directors for astronomical amounts (albeit, the case settled for far less while on appeal). The Japanese legislature reacted by amending the Japanese Commercial Code to allow corporations to include provisions in their charters limiting the directors' liability for damages—except for acts not done in good faith or which involve gross negligence—to a multiple of the directors' annual compensation. The amendment also allows the board of directors to pass a resolution waiving liability, but any shareholder(s) holding 3% of the corporation's shares may challenge such a board voted waiver. Shoho [Commercial Code], art. 266(7)–266(23). At first glance, this action appears to illustrate how law spreads between different nations when legislatures are confronted with similar events. Compare, however, the Japanese statute with Delaware's Section 102(b)(7). Are there some critical differences? Would it have made sense for the Delaware legislature to exclude gross negligence from the permissible reach of exculpatory charter provisions as a reaction to *Van Gorkom*? Why did this make sense in response to the *Daiwa* decision? Also, the idea of capping damages at a multiple of director compensation is not in Section 102(b)(7). Where did this come from? Finally, what is the practical impact of the ability of directors to waive liability unless shareholder(s) holding 3% of the stock object? Compare this impact with the law in those nations that only allow derivative suits by shareholders holding a certain minimum percentage of stock.

5. The actions brought by government officials seeking civil (*Barings*) or criminal (*Mannesmann*) sanctions against directors accused of mismanagement suggest another approach. Of course, criminal prosecutions of corporate officials in cases of grievous misappropriation of corporate assets happen in the United States—witness the recent prosecution of officials of Tyco Corporation. Also, United States securities laws allow the Securities Exchange Commission to disqualify individuals from serving as directors of public corporations when their conduct "demonstrates substantial unfitness to serve as an officer or director" of an issuer. 15 U.S.C. § 77t(e). Compare

this provision (enacted in 1990) with the English Director Disqualification Act of 1986, which, as discussed in *Barings*, allows disqualification of directors for unfitness. In any event, might one suspect that public enforcement actions (either civil or criminal) have greater significance, if not greater frequency, in jurisdictions in which there is less private enforcement through derivative suits?

6.   In examining the efficacy of either private or official actions against those accused of mismanaging a corporation, one should be aware of the broader context created by a nation's judicial system. For example, consider the impact of a loser-pays rule for the award of attorneys fees, or a prohibition on contingency fees, on the willingness of a shareholder with a small stake in the corporation to bring a derivative suit. Consider the impact of limited discovery rules generally prevailing outside the United States on the viability of private actions against directors or controlling shareholders based upon a strong suspicion, but no firm proof, of mismanagement. Recall also the caveat expressed in the Wall Street Journal article about Mexico's new securities law in which the writer reports that traditionally there has been little prosecution of white collar crimes in Mexico.

Chapter VI

INSIDER TRADING

Unlike robbery or bribery, there has been no longstanding or universal condemnation among human civilizations of transacting business based upon inside information. Indeed, the United States appears to have been the first country to prohibit trading by corporate insiders on inside information—and that only in the early 1960s—followed a few years later by France. Prohibitions on trading on inside information really began to spread among nations in the 1980s and, especially, in the 1990s, such that, by 2000, 87 countries had adopted laws prohibiting trading on inside information. Utpal Bhattacharya & Hazem Daouk, *The World Price of Insider Trading*, 57 J. Fin. 75 (2002). This chapter explores why this prohibition spread, and a few of the differences in the way in which other nations define the prohibited conduct.

FRANKLIN A. GEVURTZ, THE GLOBALIZATION OF INSIDER TRADING PROHIBITIONS

15 Transnat'l Law. 63 (2002).

* * *

Several events contributed to this growth [in the number of nations prohibiting trading on inside information]. * * * The fall of the iron curtain and the development of market economies in the formerly socialist economies of Eastern Europe led to the spread of stock markets. This, in turn, led some nations, who previously had little reason for concern over insider trading (since they had little or no stock trading in any event), to enact insider trading prohibitions. Yet, this explanation covers only a small part of the story. While the 1990s witnessed a significant increase in the number of countries with stock markets, the number of nations with insider trading regulations grew much more rapidly. As a result, the world went from a situation, at the start of the 1990s, in which the majority of countries with stock markets did not prohibit insider trading, to a situation in which the overwhelming majority of countries with stock markets had enacted such a prohibition by the year 2000.

* * *

Several forces seem to have led to the dramatic recent growth in insider trading prohibitions even among nations which already had stock markets. One force may be simply instinctive imitation spawned by the growing cultural and economic dominance of the United States at the close of the Twentieth Century. In other words, the spread of insider trading prohibitions might reflect nothing more rational than the securities law mirror of the spread of American Rock-and-Roll, Levi's Jeans, and McDonald's hamburgers. Indeed, the timing of the spread of insider trading prohibitions lends credence to this explanation. The 1980s witnessed highly publicized insider trading prosecutions in the United States. The important agent of dispersing American culture, Hollywood, did its part to vilify insider trading at about this time in the movie *Wall Street*. As a result, instances of insider trading outside the United States—such as a 1987 incident involving Hashin Sogo Bank's disposal of its shares in Tatecho Chemical Industries the day before the Japanese chemical company publicly announced massive losses—which, in an earlier time, might have passed without comment, generated significant publicity and calls for action [against insider trading in Japan].

Of course, governments are hardly going to adopt insider trading prohibitions based upon the express rationale that if American Rock-and-Roll is good, so must be American style insider trading prohibitions. Moreover, a rationale that the government should make insider trading illegal because the conduct is unfair and immoral raises the question as to why, if this is the case, the law, for so many years, had allowed the conduct. Hence, it is not surprising that the express rationale in many countries for making insider trading illegal looks to pragmatic economic considerations. Specifically, nations around the world have sought to increase the depth and liquidity of their local stock markets to match the sort of depth and liquidity found on the New York Stock Exchange. The hope is that the broader investor base promoted by such markets would lower the cost of capital for local corporations, thereby aiding the ability of local corporations to compete in the global economy. * * * Governments have come to believe that among the regulations necessary * * * for deep and liquid stock markets is a ban on at least some amount of trading on inside information.

* * *

Determining whether insider trading prohibitions will achieve the economic goal of promoting deep and liquid stock markets and a lower cost of capital is a much more complex question.

* * *

It is an oversimplification to suggest that people will not invest in stock if they fear becoming the victim of another person's trading on inside information. * * * [H]owever, * * * rational investors should demand a higher rate of return when investing in stock, in order to compensate for the risk of being on the wrong end of a trade based upon inside information. * * *

* * * One way to reduce the risk of being on the wrong end of an insider trade is to become an insider. For instance, individuals or institutions holding substantial percentages of a corporation's outstanding stock (so-called large blockholders) often have the clout to obtain access to corporate information (perhaps through a seat on the board). Accordingly, worries about insider trading would seem more salient to the small investor than to the large blockholder. Moreover, small investors often end up putting their money to work in corporations even if small investors do not buy stock. For example, small investors worried about insider trading can put their money into a bank. The bank, in turn, can use its depositors' money to finance corporations through loans or, if allowed under the jurisdiction's banking laws, by taking equity positions. This analysis suggests that the fear of insider trading may not reduce the total financing available to corporations, nor even necessarily lead investors to demand a higher return on stock purchases. Instead, it might serve to promote large block holdings in corporations, with small investors putting their money only indirectly into corporate businesses.

This discussion of the differential impact of insider trading on large blockholders and small investors has a couple of implications. To begin with, it might help explain why German banks were a major source of the opposition to adoption of Germany's insider trading law. More fundamentally, this differential impact brings into focus the relationship between insider trading and broader issues of comparative corporate governance and finance. Specifically, much recent scholarship in corporate governance and finance has focused on the fact that large blockholders commonly dominate the ownership of major corporations outside the United States; in other words, a relatively small number of institutions or individuals commonly own a majority of any given foreign corporation's stock. * * * To the extent that dominance by large blockholders is more efficient than widely dispersed ownership, or, without respect to efficiency, a variety of intractable forces will preserve large blockholder dominance in non-American corporations, then it could be undesirable or futile to prohibit insider trading outside the United States in the hope that this will increase direct ownership of stock by small investors.

* * *

[For example,] Professors Bratton and McCahery [have argued] * * * that prohibitions on insider trading in nations with large blockholder dominance might only lead to more self-dealing by such large blockholders, with the result that small investors still shy away from owning stock.[1]

1. [William Bratton & Joseph McCahery, *Comparative Corporate Governance and the Theory of the Firm: The Case Against* *Global Cross Reference*, 38 Colum. J. Transnat'l L. 213 (1999)] at 294–295.

Ultimately, however, the question of whether insider trading prohibitions will promote deep and liquid markets, and decrease the cost of capital, should yield an empirical answer. A recent study by Professors Bhattacharya and Daouk suggests that there is some positive news in this regard. By using four sets of available statistics, which the two professors contend can serve as surrogates for the cost of capital in a nation, Professors Bhattacharya and Daouk examined whether insider trading laws decreased the cost of capital in the nations around the world that have enacted such laws. They found that the enactment of insider trading prohibitions produced no statistically significant impact. However, they also found that a statistically significant improvement in the cost of capital in a nation occurred after the first prosecution took place under the nation's insider trading laws. In other words, while mere enactment of insider trading laws apparently produces no impact on investor confidence, efforts to enforce the law do.

* * *

Note

As an illustration of the relationships between insider trading, self-dealing, concentrated ownership of corporate stock, and the difference between enacting and enforcing insider trading prohibitions, review the Wall Street Journal article on Mexico's new securities law, excerpted in Chapter V. In fact, the reporter seems to have gotten the story wrong (shocking) in describing the Salinas transaction in debt instruments issued by Unefon (a company Salinas controlled). According to the complaint filed by the Securities Exchange Commission against Salinas, Salinas' shell company did *not* buy Unefon debt for pennies on the dollar *from Unefon*, in order to resell the debt back to Unefon a few months later at face value. Rather, Salinas' shell company purchased the debt at a deep discount from a third party creditor of Unefon—while Salinas knew, unlike the creditor, that Unefon would be getting an infusion of cash that would allow Unefon to pay off, rather than default on, the debt. In other words, this case allegedly involved profiting on inside information, rather than unfair self-dealing. From the standpoint of encouraging investment in Mexican corporations, does this difference matter? Would Salinas' alleged action constitute unlawful insider trading under United States law? Under the insider trading laws of other nations?

DIRECTIVE 2003/6/EC OF THE EUROPEAN PARLIA- MENT AND OF THE COUNCIL AS REGARDS THE DEFINITION AND PUBLIC DISCLOSURE OF IN- SIDE INFORMATION AND THE DEFINITION OF MARKET MANIPULATION

2003 O.J. (L339) 70.

* * *

Article 1

For the purposes of this Directive:

1. 'Inside information' shall mean information of a precise nature which has not been made public, relating, directly or indirectly, to one or

more issuers of financial instruments or to one or more financial instruments and which, if it were made public, would be likely to have a significant effect on the prices of those financial instruments or on the price of related derivative financial instruments.

* * *

3. 'Financial instrument' shall mean:

—transferable securities as defined in Council Directive 93/22/EEC of 10 May 1993

* * *

—options to acquire or dispose of any instrument falling into these categories

* * *

—any other instrument admitted to trading on a regulated market in a Member State or for which a request for admission to trading on such a market has been made.

* * *

Article 2

1. Member States shall prohibit any person referred to in the second subparagraph who possesses inside information from using that information by acquiring or disposing of, or by trying to acquire or dispose of, for his own account or for the account of a third party, either directly or indirectly, financial instruments to which that information relates.

2. The first subparagraph shall apply to any person who possesses that information:

(a) by virtue of his membership of the administrative, management or supervisory bodies of the issuer; or

(b) by virtue of his holding in the capital of the issuer; or

(c) by virtue of his having access to the information through the exercise of his employment, profession or duties; or

(d) by virtue of his criminal activities.

* * *

3. This Article shall not apply to transactions conducted in the discharge of an obligation that has become due to acquire or dispose of financial instruments where that obligation results from an agreement concluded before the person concerned possessed inside information.

Article 3

Member States shall prohibit any person subject to the prohibition laid down in Article 2 from:

(a) disclosing inside information to any other person unless such disclosure is made in the normal course of the exercise of his employment, profession or duties;

(b) recommending or inducing another person, on the basis of inside information, to acquire or dispose of financial instruments to which that information relates.

Article 4

Member States shall ensure that Articles 2 and 3 also apply to any person, other than the persons referred to in those Articles, who possesses inside information while that person knows, or ought to have known, that it is inside information.

* * *

Article 6

1. Member States shall ensure that issuers of financial instruments inform the public as soon as possible of inside information which directly concerns the said issuers. * * *

2. An issuer may under his own responsibility delay the public disclosure of inside information, as referred to in paragraph 1, such as not to prejudice his legitimate interests provided that such omission would not be likely to mislead the public and provided that the issuer is able to ensure the confidentiality of that information. * * *

3. Member States shall require that, whenever an issuer, or a person acting on his behalf or for his account, discloses any inside information to any third party in the normal exercise of his employment, profession or duties, as referred to in Article 3(a), he must make complete and effective public disclosure of that information, simultaneously in the case of an intentional disclosure and promptly in the case of a non-intentional disclosure.

The provisions of the first subparagraph shall not apply if the person receiving the information owes a duty of confidentiality, regardless of whether such duty is based on a law, on regulations, on articles of association or on a contract.

* * *

Article 10

Each Member State shall apply the prohibitions and requirements provided for in this Directive to:

(a) actions carried out on its territory or abroad concerning financial instruments that are admitted to trading on a regulated market situated or operating within its territory or for which a request for admission to trading on such market has been made;

(b) actions carried out on its territory concerning financial instruments that are admitted to trading on a regulated market in a Member State or for which a request for admission to trading on such market has been made.

* * *

Notes

1. Consider the jurisdictional reach of the European Union insider trading prohibition as mandated by the directive in Article 10(a). Suppose a person in the United States, while possessing inside information as defined under the directive, enters into a contract to purchase or sell stock traded on a European exchange (say shares in Daimler–Chrysler AG): Would German law following the directive reach this person's action, even if he or she entered the contract in the United States? If so, what does this say about the need for lawyers in the United States to be aware of European Union insider trading law?

2. Examine Articles 2 and 4 of the directive. At first glance, they appear to represent an inexplicably pointless combination: Article 2 lists certain categories of persons who cannot trade based upon inside information, while Article 4 in effect says "never mind the categories," no one, for the most part, can trade based upon inside information.

In fact, this seemingly odd drafting is the result of the historical development of the directive. The European Council originally issued its insider trading directive in 1989. Article 2 of the current version of the directive is a continuation of Article 2 in the 1989 directive (except that Article 2 in the current directive added more one category—persons acquiring information by criminal activities—to the list of those who could not trade based on inside information). Article 4, as it existed in the 1989 directive, prohibited trading based on inside information by so-called secondary insiders—which was anyone who received information directly or indirectly from persons listed in Article 2 (which, in turn, were called primary insiders). The current directive (issued in 2003) changed Article 4 to get rid of the limitation that the information must come from a person listed in Article 2, thereby making anyone trading on inside information subject to the prohibition regardless of where the information originated. At this point, the only purpose for retaining the Article 2 categories is to distinguish persons who may assert that they did not realize they were trading on inside information from those for whom such an argument is legally irrelevant.

In order to assess the significance of the new directive, as well as to appreciate how both versions of the directive differ from United States law, compare what the outcome would have been if the directive (both as originally issued in 1989 and in its current form) had applied in the following cases:

Chiarella v. United States, 445 U.S. 222 (1980) (reversing the conviction of the employee of a printing company, who acquired the identity of takeover targets by virtue of his job printing confidential documents for companies making the tender offers, when the conviction was based upon an instruction that the jury should convict if it simply found the defendant traded upon material non-public information)

Dirks v. Securities Exchange Commission, 463 U.S. 646 (1983) (reversing the censure of a securities analyst, who passed on information he received from a former insider, when the insider did not personally benefit from giving the analyst the tip)

SEC v. Switzer, 590 F.Supp. 756 (W.D. Okla. 1984) (held that a coach, who overheard a conversation between insiders at a football game, did not break the law by trading based upon the information)

3.   While the insider trading prohibition in the European Union directive is more expansive than the law in the United States, Japan provides an example of a law that is narrower. The Japanese prohibition reaches socalled corporate related parties. This includes directors, officers, employees, shareholders, as well as persons associated with a corporation through either a contract or a government supervisory role, who obtain material non-public information by virtue of their relationship with the company. Such corporate related parties cannot trade, while in possession of material non-public information, stock of the corporation to which they have a relation, or stock of another company which is subject to a planned tender offer by the corporation to which they have a relation. Shoken torihikiho [Securities and Exchange Law], art. 190–2, 190–3 (as amended in 1988).

This prohibition is narrower than United States law in a couple of potentially significant ways. To begin with, Japanese law only prohibits trading by persons who gain information that comes, directly or indirectly, from the corporation in whose stock they trade or a corporation making a tender offer for the stock they trade—in other words, there is no equivalent to the United States misappropriation doctrine. Compare the outcome this produces under Japanese law with the result in *Carpenter v. United States*, 484 U.S. 19 (1987) (the court held that trading stocks based on the advance knowledge of the contents of a newspaper column, which discussed the stocks, in breach of the reporter's duty to the newspaper, constituted mail and wire fraud).

Moreover, the Japanese statute does not prohibit tipping. Instead, the only way in which the Japanese law deals with tipping is by punishing persons who receive information directly from an corporate insider and who trade (in other words, only the first-tier tippee who trades is liable). Consider the outcome this would produce under Japanese law in the situation facing the United States Supreme Courts in *Dirks, supra* (an investment analyst received information from a corporate insider and passed on the inside information to his clients, but did not trade himself, while the clients traded based upon the information). What outcome does this produce under Japanese law even if the insider in *Dirks* had sold the analyst the information, rather than giving the information to the analyst in the hope of exposing a fraud?

This raises the question of why the Japanese followed the approach laid out above. In fact, the Japanese law bares a similarity to what one would get if one took the narrowest view of the insider trading prohibition under United States securities law in 1988, made a few changes (as in the way Japanese law deals with tipping) to simplify litigation, and added a provision (specifically, picking up parties who gain inside information by virtue of a contract with the corporation in whose stock they trade) to deal with the precise scandal that provoked the law. All told, might this be the reaction of a government that was not sure how much it really wanted to enact an insider trading prohibition, but felt political pressure to do so after an insider trading scandal?

4.   Another way to deal with insider trading is to reduce the amount of inside information by increasing corporate disclosure. Notice how the European Council directive attempts to accomplish this. Compare the directive with the move toward more continuous disclosure obligations in the United States through the Sarbanes–Oxley Act and with Regulation FD.

Chapter VII

TAKEOVERS

Before the 1960s, the subject of corporate takeovers around the world was largely a study in friendly transactions—in the sense that the board of directors of the company taken over supported the acquisition. As a result, legal disputes about corporate takeovers were less frequent, and typically involved the rights of shareholders who dissented from the transaction or complained that they did not equally share in its rewards. The business cultural norm against taking over a corporation in the face opposition by its existing board of directors (a hostile takeover) started to change first in the United States, such that, by the 1980s, epic takeover contests in the United States had turned this topic into an important focus of corporate law development. For some time, the hostile takeover remained largely a United States' phenomenon, and the persistence of a business culture resistant to the hostile takeover appeared to mark a major divergence between corporate practice inside and outside of the United States. It now appears, however, rather than marking a persistent divergence between the United States and other nations, that the presence of the hostile takeover is a wave phenomenon, which struck the United States first and has since spread to other parts of the world. The result is to allow for an exploration of some very different legal responses to the hostile takeover.

MARCO VENTORUZZO, EUROPE'S THIRTEENTH DIRECTIVE AND U.S. TAKEOVER REGULATION: REGULATORY MEANS AND POLITICAL AND ECONOMIC ENDS

41 Tex. Int'l L. Rev. 171 (2006).

I. Introduction

* * * In something of a surprise twist for many observers of corporate affairs, European multinationals dominate American corporations in numerous strategic industries, and European corporations are taking over American corporations at a higher rate than American corporations are reciprocating.

* * *

132

European and U.S. approaches to takeover regulation are strikingly different in their content and even their philosophical approaches. The recently enacted Thirteenth Directive represents an important step because, as it attempts to harmonize national rules in Europe, it also confirms and exacerbates the divergence of the regulatory paths followed by Europe and the United States in this area of the law.

* * *

IV.   The European Approach to Takeover Regulation

* * *

A.   *The Founding Principles*

* * * Somewhat surprisingly given the existence of profound historical, legal and cultural differences among the several European countries, most of the takeover laws (in particular those of France, Germany, Italy, Spain and the United Kingdom, as well as the European Union's Thirteenth Directive) share a common overall structure. * * *

Following the U.K. experience, most European countries required compulsory tender offers on all outstanding shares when a specified controlling threshold was acquired * * *. There are two rationales for adopting a compulsory public offer regime. On the one hand, the technique is designed to favor the distribution of the controlling premium to a large group of investors.

* * *

A second goal of compulsory tender offers * * * is to provide a fair opportunity for minority shareholders to exit in the event of an undesirable change in the controlling shareholder.

* * *

These provisions may be particularly desirable in a market that is regarded as not particularly "thick" or efficient, meaning a market in which control of listed corporations is often transferred outside the market, through friendly transactions among insiders able to capitalize control premiums to the detriment of minority investors. This risk is particularly high in corporations with strong controlling shareholders and concentrated ownership structures, a condition present, to varying degrees, in most continental European countries.

* * *

The second founding principle of the European takeover regime deals with limitations to the defensive measures that a target company can implement to resist hostile acquisitions through public offers. An unfriendly acquisition raises a conflict of interest between the incumbents controlling the corporation and, in particular, the directors, [versus] * * * the shareholders. The U.S. system addresses this conflict of interest mainly through the fiduciary duties owed by the directors to the shareholders, holding them liable in cases of breach of their duties of loyalty or of care, as developed in takeover case law. On the contrary, the European approach freezes directors' powers once a public offer has been launched and requires any action that might adversely affect the outcome of the takeover to be approved by the shareholders. In addition, some poison pills that might not require any action from the directors, but still prevent the takeover and jeopardize the interests of minority shareholders, are temporarily neutralized through the so-called "breakthrough rule."

In brief, it might be said that the European approach directly empowers shareholders on the issue of defensive measures. The desirability of this approach must be considered in light of the peculiar ownership patterns that prevail in Europe[, specifically, concentrated block holding even in large corporations], since it might be argued that Europe has simply replaced the conflict between directors and shareholders with that between controlling and minority shareholders.

B.   *Takeover Regulation in Some European States*

* * *

1.   Compulsory Tender Offer Rules

The origins of compulsory [tender offers] * * * can be found in the British City Code, which is not a statutory provision but is mandatory in the sense that there are specific sanctions in the case of noncompliance. The Code provides that whoever acquires over 30 percent of the outstanding voting shares of a public corporation must launch a public offer on all the remaining shares at a price not lower than the highest price paid for the same shares in the last twelve months.

* * *

[Following the example of the British experience with the City Code on takeovers, several large European countries, such as France, Germany, Italy and Spain, have adopted compulsory tender offer rules.]

3.   Board Neutrality and the Breakthrough Rule

Most legal systems that mandate compulsory tender offers also impose a passivity or neutrality rule. Once again, the rule is inspired by the British model. The City Code's General Principle 7 provides that:

> At no time a bona fide offer has been communicated to the board of the offeree company, or after the board of the offeree company has reason to believe that a bona fide offer might be imminent, may any action be taken by the board of the offeree company in relation to the affairs of the company, without the approval of the shareholders in general meeting, which could effectively result in any bona fide offer being frustrated or in the shareholders being denied an opportunity to decide on its merits.

Rule 21 enumerates specific defensive measures that cannot be adopted without shareholder consent, such as issuing previously authorized shares, selling assets of material value, or entering into important contractual relationships. The passivity rule applies, obviously, both in case of voluntary and of compulsory tender offers; and independently from the friendly or hostile nature of the bid.

Applying the passivity rule might raise several delicate problems of interpretation. It could be said that every action that might de facto frustrate the bid is prohibited from being adopted or at least implemented unilaterally by the directors, even if they received some pre-bid authorization from the shareholders' meeting. It is not, however, always easy to distinguish actions that might have this effect. In any case, the rationale of the rule is that the shareholders, as the primary recipients of the offer, shall decide on the adoption of any defensive strategy or tactic, only after the offer has been made and in the light of all the information available.

* * *

The German approach, which is also followed in The Netherlands, presents a slightly different scheme that makes defensive measures comparatively easy to adopt. At first blush, the prohibition against actions inimical to the tender offer * * * provided for by section 33, 1 (1) of the [German] Takeover Act, the WpÜG, follows the U.K. approach and bans directors' defenses unapproved by the shareholders' meeting. However, section 33, 1 (2) of the WpÜG provides that the members of the managing board * * * can also adopt defensive measures approved by the supervisory board * * *. While the members of this latter body, which is separately appointed at the shareholders' meeting, have some independence requirements vis-à-vis the members of the [management board], they are nevertheless directors who are appointed by the existing majority. As such, their interests can conflict with those of minority shareholders in opposing value-maximizing hostile offers that might jeopardize their positions within the corporation. This potential for conflict is exacerbated when the members of the [supervisory board] are also appointed by the unions, as is required by statute in larger corporations. As a general matter, unions tend to oppose proposed acquisitions that might result in reorganizations and downsize the number of employees, regardless of the desirability of the offer from the shareholders' point of view.

In addition, in contrast to the strict neutrality rule followed in most continental European countries, under German law the shareholders' meeting can release a preliminary general authorization * * * to the directors to amend the corporate bylaws. * * * Authorization before the bid is a sort of blank check to the directors, since it is given without information on the conditions of the bid.

C.   The Thirteenth Directive on Takeovers

* * *

1.   The Long and Winding Road to Passage

Discussion of harmonized regulation of takeovers began in Europe in the late 1980s, partially as a consequence of one of the first attempts at a cross-border hostile takeover. In 1988, the Italian entrepreneur Carlo De Benedetti launched a hostile takeover of the Belgian corporation Société Générale de Belgique. The attempt was ultimately thwarted by an acquisition by a French white knight, but it highlighted the growing concern in Europe about an unregulated no-man's land in such a delicate field. In 1989, European authorities responded by elaborating a first proposal for a Directive on takeovers.

The proposal was probably premature given the political climate and it was turned down.* * * In 1996, after further discussion, a proposal for a directive based on the principles set down by the British City Code was [promulgated]. This proposal, which also received strenuous opposition, contained the two principle pillars of the U.K. approach: compulsory bids and board neutrality.

Once again, the call for intensifying the efforts to reach a common position and adopt a harmonized regulatory framework was, at least partially, prompted by an international acquisition that underlined the desirability of a shared regulatory framework. In 1999, a U.K. telecommunications corporation, Vodafone, successfully completed the hostile takeover of the German colossus Mannesmann. The battle over this important and strategic enterprise attracted significant political attention as the prime ministers of the two countries, Tony Blair and Gerhard Schröeder, intervened (according to some improperly) by commenting on the desirability and effects of the takeover. In June 2000, a common position for a harmonized regulation that might create a level-playing field was reached, but substantial critiques had still been raised, especially against the neutrality rule.

In July 2001, the proposal was presented to the European Parliament, but ended in a deadlock 273 to 273. For lack of a single vote, the proposal was rejected, mainly due to the opposition of the German members of Parliament.

* * *

Finally, a new proposal * * * was presented to the European Parliament in October 2002. After extensive further discussion, the Thirteenth Directive was finally approved on April 21, 2004. The text that was adopted represents a positive innovation in terms of harmonization, but is in many ways a compromise that diluted previous projects by leaving significant regulatory freedom to national legislatures.

* * *

2. The Pillars of the Directive

The Thirteenth Directive is a very complex piece of legislation, addressing several aspects of takeover regulation, from the information that should be disclosed, to instances when it is permissible to cash out minority shareholders; from the regulation of employees' rights, to the issue of regulatory competence for cross-border transactions. My analysis will focus on the pillars of the European approach: mandatory bids, board neutrality and the breakthrough rule.

Article 5(1) of the Directive requires compulsory offers when natural or legal persons, acting alone or in concert with others, acquire a certain threshold of ownership in the corporation's securities (meaning transferable securities of corporations carrying voting rights regulated by the law of a Member State and listed on a regulated European market). Specifically, if newly acquired shares:

> added to any existing holdings of those securities of his/hers and the holdings of those securities of persons acting in concert with him/her, directly or indirectly give him/her a specified percentage of voting rights in that company, giving him/her control of that company, Member States shall ensure that such a person is required to make a bid as a means of protecting the minority shareholders of that company. Such a bid shall be addressed at the earliest opportunity to all the holders of those securities for all their holdings at the equitable price as defined in paragraph 4.

Under this provision, the triggering event mandating the public offer is the acquisition by one or more persons acting together of a percentage of securities, and therefore voting rights, that give the bidder control over the corporation. The Directive neither defines control, nor provides, in contrast to the individual national legislation described above, a fixed threshold representing a presumption of control.

This very crucial element of takeover regulation is intentionally left to the discretion of Member States. According to paragraph 3 of Article 5:

> "The percentage of voting rights which confers control for the purposes of paragraph 1 and the method of its calculation shall be determined by the rules of the Member State in which the company has its registered office."

This is one of the many compromises that the harmonization process had to accept, which allows the individual national legislatures to adopt different provisions regarding the threshold of participation triggering the compulsory bid. * * *

3. The Price of the Compulsory Tender Offer

Another crucial element of the compulsory bid is its price. Also in this respect the Directive is very flexible. Article 5, paragraph 4 provides:

> The highest price paid for the same securities by the offeror, or by persons acting in concert with him/her, over a period, to be determined by Member States, of not less than six months and not more than 12 before the bid referred to in paragraph 1 shall be regarded as the equitable price.

* * *

Also with respect to this element, however, the Directive leaves significant freedom to Member States. The second section of paragraph 4 of Article 5, allows them to "authorise their supervisory authorities to adjust the price" particularly "in circumstances and in accordance with criteria that are clearly determined." * * *

4.   Board Neutrality

With respect to board neutrality, as with most European countries, the Directive follows the British approach described above by mandating that the board remain neutral in its actions. The Directive also requires that the board of the target corporation publish a statement of its evaluation of the offer and its possible effects, including its effects on employment levels and on the relocation of company activities. More precisely, when a bid is launched, whether it is voluntary of compulsory, the directors of the target corporation cannot take any action that might frustrate the bid and in particular—according to article 9(2)—issue "any shares which may result in a lasting impediment to the offeror's acquiring control of the offeree company." These actions can be pursued only via shareholder authorization.

* * *

Another delicate issue concerns the ability of the shareholders to grant prior authorization to adopt and implement certain defensive measures to the board in case of a takeover, at a time when no offer has been (yet) launched on the corporation. As discussed in the previous pages, the German Takeover Act of 2002 provided for a similar possibility * * *.

In this respect, Article 9 of the directive requires a specific authorization given by the shareholders during the relevant period in which the offer is public as a condition for the adoption of any defensive action. * * *

The neutrality rule, however, is not applicable to actions that are "part of the normal course of the company's business." This notion presents some ambiguities, which might leave enough room to national legislatures, or to the parties involved in the contest, to let directors implement some actions that serve or have the effect of undermining the bid, relying only on a shareholders' decision given before the bid was public. In any case, the difficulty in distinguishing the corporation's "normal course of business" from extraordinary measures taken to frustrate a bid might lead to inefficient litigation.

5.   The Breakthrough Rule

The neutrality rule deals with defensive measures that require the directors to take some specific actions to repel hostile offers. A corporation or its controlling shareholders can, however, adopt certain provisions designed to entrench control, or at least make a successful hostile offer much less likely to succeed, which can operate without any specific action when the takeover is initiated. Examples of such provisions include the issuance of dual-class share structures with multiple voting shares in the hands of a blockholder; shareholders' agreements that limit the free transferability of shares; supermajority requirements to approve the corporate transactions often required after a takeover (such as a merger); golden parachutes for directors or top executives triggered by events linked to an unwelcome change in control. Even the very existence of classes of shares with different voting rights can act as an impediment to takeovers. These measures share certain essential features and functions with U.S.-style poison pills * * *.

The European legislature, again following the examples of some national regulations, has provided for a "breakthrough rule." The rule is intended to neutralize some of these anti-takeover devices in the event of a hostile offer. In the European scenario, the rule has two major goals. The first and obvious purpose is to limit the ability of the controlling group to entrench its position and fend off efficient offers. More importantly, however, the purpose of this regulation is to create a leveled-playing field across Europe. The various systems of corporate law, regulated at the Member State level, provide for different rules concerning defensive devices. For example, some countries allow listed corporations to issue multi-voting shares, or for shareholders to devise agreements limiting share transferability, which are either disallowed or regulated more stringently in other States. * * * The breakthrough rule, therefore, was designed * * * to mitigate, at least in the context of a takeover, these differences.

* * *

Article 11 provides for two different situations in which the breakthrough rule applies. The first is when a bid is made public. In this instance, any restriction on the transfer of securities or on the exercise of voting rights, either provided in the bylaws of the target corporation or in contractual agreements among shareholders, is rendered ineffective until the end of the offer. By way of example, a preemptive right enjoyed by shareholding members of the controlling group would be neutralized under Article 11. Instead of being bound to offer the shares to other shareholders before selling them to third parties, individual shareholders could tender them to the bidder without liability for contractual breach. Under Article 11, the launch of a tender offer, in other words, releases everybody from previous engagements in order to favor efficient share allocation.

In addition, after the offer has been completed, if it has been particularly successful (i.e., more than three quarters of the outstanding voting shares have been tendered), pursuant to paragraph 4 of Article 11, the offeror can call a shareholders' meeting to appoint new directors or to amend the corporate articles of incorporation and/or bylaws. In that event, no preexisting restrictions, such as voting caps, multiple voting rights, supermajority requirements, and the like, apply. This part of the rule is designed to sterilize those defenses that would operate ex post, once the new controlling shareholder steps in to reorganize the corporation or simply to replace its top executives. In contrast with U.S.

law, the breakthrough principle can be seen as a device designed to curtail anti-takeover statutes and poison pills and related mechanisms that limit the market for corporate control.

* * *

6.   Real Harmonization?

* * *

The irony of this supposed harmonization is that, as to [board neutrality and the breakthrough rule] * * *, the supposed imposition of new law by the European legislature is really a recommendation. Article 12 of the Directive states:

> Member States may reserve the right not to require companies ... which have their registered offices within their territories to apply Article 9(2) and (3) [encompassing the board passivity directive] and/or Article 11 [the breakthrough rule]. . . .

* * *

Notes

1.   Professor Ventoruzzo identifies two policies behind the compulsory tender offer. One is to ensure that all stockholders benefit equally per share in any takeover premium, rather than allowing controlling stockholders to obtain more for each of their shares than minority stockholders. Is this equal benefit notion completely foreign to law in the United States? See *Perlman v. Feldmann*, 219 F.2d 173 (2d Cir. 1955); *Jones v. H.F. Ahmanson & Co.*, 1 Cal. 3d 93, 81 Cal. Rptr. 592, 460 P.2d 464 (1969). Is there some reason that most courts in the United States have rejected an equal benefit obligation?

The second policy behind the compulsory tender offer is to allow minority stockholders to bail out in the event control passes to a stockholder they might not like. This addresses one justification often urged in support of the incumbent board instituting a defense to a hostile tender offer: the need to protect minority stockholders from being coerced into tendering their shares for fear of remaining trapped in the corporation at the mercy of a new controlling stockholder. In fact, based upon this rationale, compulsory tender offer rules exist in the United States in some state takeover laws, and in individual corporations through so-called "Fair Price Amendments" found in some corporate articles, and through the provisions of some poison pill plans.

2.   While the English, and now European, prohibition on defensive measures without contemporaneous shareholder approval is not the law anywhere in the United States, some United States corporate law scholars early on advocated such a rule. Easterbrook & Fischel, *The Proper Role of a Target's Management in Responding to a Tender Offer*, 94 Harv. L. Rev. 1161 (1981).

One practical problem with a board neutrality rule is figuring out what constitutes a defense to a tender offer—since all sorts of business decisions and corporate financial and governance structures, including decisions and structures implemented long before a tender offer was on the scene—can make a company less attractive to an acquirer. Notice how the London City Code and the Thirteenth Directive attempt to deal with this.

On a policy level, what is the purpose of a board neutrality rule? How does corporate law in United States (especially Delaware) attempt to achieve the same objective? Is there some reason why law in the United States has looked to judicial enforcement of fiduciary duty as the principal answer to the danger that directors will place their own interest in retaining power over the interest of the shareholders in getting a good deal, while law in Europe has moved to a categorical statutory rule? Does this difference in overall approach ring a familiar bell?

Professor Ventoruzzo suggests that shifting power to the stockholders to vote on takeover defenses will substitute a conflict between controlling versus minority stockholders for a conflict between directors versus stockholders. Do controlling shareholders need to worry about takeover defenses?

What about the interests of other stakeholders in the corporation, such as employees, whom a takeover might impact? Does a board neutrality rule prevent the directors from taking defensive steps against a tender offer that might threaten the employees' jobs? In this light, does it seem odd that Europe, in which stakeholder interests appear to receive more protection than in the United States, has adopted a board neutrality rule? Might the existence of other protections for stakeholder interests, such as co-determination, mean that there is less justification for boards to fend off takeovers based upon the rationale of protecting corporate stakeholders?

3. Professor Ventoruzzo states that the perceived need for a "level playing field" among different European nations when it comes to cross-border takeovers provided a critical motivation for the Thirteenth Directive. The concern is that a government in a country (say, France) might take actions to prevent foreign corporations taking over key local companies, at the same time this country supports efforts by its own corporations to take over foreign companies. Is this a concern for the United States? If so, what, if anything, will be the impact of an un-level playing field when it comes to cross-border corporate takeovers between the United States and Europe as a result of the difference in takeover laws? In any event, to what extent has the Thirteenth Directive succeeded in creating a level playing field as far as takeover defenses in Europe?

4. Defying stereotypes, hostile takeovers recently also have come to Japan. The response of Japanese lawmakers (both judicial and administrative) has been to adopt Delaware rather than European rules. For a discussion of why the Japanese followed this route—suggesting that it was not because of the superiority of Delaware law for shareholder protection—see Curtis J. Milhaupt, *In the Shadow of Delaware? The Rise of Hostile Takeovers in Japan*, 105 Colum. L. Rev. 2171 (2005).

*

Index

References are to Pages

†